THE DIY GUIDE TO
MAKING MUSIC VIDEOS
FOR THE INDEPENDENT MUSICIAN

BY JON FORSYTH

To access photos and videos, visit:
www.halleonard.com/mylibrary

Enter Code
7714-7854-4228-9269

ISBN 978-1-5400-3532-5

HAL•LEONARD®

Visit Hal Leonard Online at
www.halleonard.com

Contact us:
Hal Leonard
7777 West Bluemound Road
Milwaukee, WI 53213
Email: info@halleonard.com

In Europe, contact:
Hal Leonard Europe Limited
42 Wigmore Street
Marylebone, London, W1U 2RN
Email: info@halleonardeurope.com

In Australia, contact:
Hal Leonard Australia Pty. Ltd.
4 Lentara Court
Cheltenham, Victoria, 3192 Australia
Email: info@halleonard.com.au

CONTENTS

ACKNOWLEDGMENTS

I'm grateful for the many factors and people that led to the completion of this book. Stephen Webber got me started on the road to Berklee and led the charge to get the teaching of music video on the program there. Berklee Valencia gave me an ideal setting for developing the curriculum and refining it over the years. Hundreds of students have inspired me to develop better ways of teaching, and continue to amaze me with their enthusiasm and creativity. Over 20 people—former students, colleagues, and some people I have never met—have contributed their thoughts and ideas to this book to make it that much better.

My wife Lori encouraged me to actually do the project, got me started and restarted at critical times, kept me going along the way, and has provided tireless editing, invaluable advice, and wonderful companionship. I'm extremely fortunate to have her with me on this journey.

INTRODUCTION

Today, music video is as necessary as recording the music in the first place. If you can't see it on YouTube, it didn't happen.

—Stephen Webber, Executive Director, BerkleeNYC

If music is your passion and you've got music ready to share, making a music video is a crucial step for spreading your creation far and wide. The process is a lot of fun and an excellent way to exercise your creativity.

The most unexpected thing about making a music video is how many people it can touch all around the world. From France to Russia or Japan or India, images are international.

—Greg et Lio, French Film Directors and Photographers

What does it take to create a great music video or even a viral music video? Can you really do it yourself (or with a few volunteer friends)?

PRO VS. DIY DIFFERENCES

The biggest differences between a professional production and do-it-yourself (DIY) videos are time, crew, and, of course, money. A professional production will generally spend a lot more time and have a much larger crew. All the crew will have training or experience, preferably both, in their respective, specialized jobs. Even though they should be efficient at what they do, they each may spend many hours to produce the advanced results they want. Since you're paying lots of professionals tens or hundreds of dollars an hour, the costs add up quickly.

A small-scale professional production could have anywhere from five to ten people working on the video, with a budget starting in the thousands of dollars. A complicated production for a big-name act might spend weeks with a crew of dozens and a budget of hundreds of thousands of dollars. (Michael Jackson holds the record for the most money spent on a music video—estimated to be $7 million at the time it was made, or over $11 million in 2019 dollars.)

A big advantage of DIY is that you can spend a lot of your own time, and arrange for (free) help from your friends. You won't have the experience of a pro, so it will be more work with more unpredictable results, but you can still have a great time and end up with an impressive product if you approach it the right way.

That's what this book is for.

Usually, more money and more professionalism add up to more views and more viral impact, but of course, there are plenty of examples of huge-budget movie productions that are box-office bombs. The same goes for music videos: lots of money doesn't guarantee success.

The reverse is also true: While there's an element of luck you can't control, the right no-budget production at the right time and place can make it big. Here are a few examples of low- or no-budget videos that gained tens of millions of views and helped kick off big music careers:

A compelling, clever visual idea: The band OK Go produced "Here We Go Again" on the cheap, and it shows. Using one camera on a tripod, with a simple tarp in the background and a few treadmills for the band to dance around on, the band filmed themselves and reportedly took 17 tries to get it right. (Over 40 million views.)

Raw talent with lots of potential: Justin Bieber got started as a pre-teen basically doing amateurish karaoke videos, sitting on his couch, singing cover songs to the camera. (Lots of lo-fi videos with hundreds of thousands or millions of views.)

Amazing musicianship with a simple setup: An early Pentatonix music video ("Somebody That I Used to Know") shows the quintet singing in what looks like an alley with some harsh shop lights and a bobbing handheld camera. (Over 60 million views.)

Music, filming, visuals all coming together: An early Lindsey Stirling video, titled simply "Epic Violin Girl," showed her unique talents with a violin, some cool visuals in an interesting location, and some smooth moves by a talented camera operator. (Over eight million views.)

And this from Laser Malena-Webber of the Doubleclicks (a nerd-folk musical duo with millions of YouTube views):

> THE BIGGEST THING I LEARNED FROM MAKING/BEING IN A MUSIC VIDEO IS THAT IT DOESN'T MATTER HOW MUCH MONEY YOU SPENT ON IT. PROJECTS WE'VE MADE FOR FREE WITH AN IPHONE HAVE WAY MORE VIEWS THAN THINGS WE'VE SPENT $500, EVEN $2,000, ON TO USE MULTIPLE FANCY CAMERAS.

PRO AND DIY SIMILARITIES: THREE BASIC STEPS

Whether you hire a professional crew to make your music video, do it yourself, or something in between, there are three basic steps in every music video creation:

1. Pre-production, or planning and preparing to film the video.

2. Production, or the actual filming.

3. Post-production, including editing, finishing, and everything else to get your video out to the world.

Here are a couple of examples of the steps involved at two extremes:

FOR JUSTIN BIEBER'S 2008 CHRIS BROWN COVER (NOT OFFICIAL, BUT MY GUESS):

1. Pre-production (15 minutes?): Decide to do the Chris Brown song. Get the backing track ready to play. Turn on the living room lights, make sure no junk is on the couch. Get somebody (friend? relative?) to hold a camera while Justin sings.

2. Production (three minutes): Record the video.

3. Post-production (10-15 minutes?): Figure out how to upload it to YouTube.

Of course, there was the audio prep work—learning the song, getting the backing track—but the audio preparation for most music videos usually happens before and separate from the music video creation.

FOR MICHAEL JACKSON'S $7-MILLION "SCREAM":

1. Pre-production (two weeks): With an A-list director (Mark Romanek), plan the logistics and hire the crew (camera, lights, set, props, costumes, hair, makeup, location, permissions, materials, etc.) for a production involving groundbreaking special effects inside a built-from-scratch futuristic spaceship that included an indoor oriental garden, a modern art gallery, and a hi-fi squash court, with seven separate sound stages in all.

2. Production (two weeks, with over one week of filming): Film all of those crazy scenes with a notoriously perfectionistic performer. (According to his sister Janet, also featured in the video, Michael spent a day just adjusting the volume of the handclaps for the audio recording.)

3. Post-production (three weeks): Scramble to get all of the editing, coloring, post-production special effects, and other fine-tuning completed (part of the reason the video was so expensive was its very tight time-schedule, given the size of the production).

IS THIS BOOK FOR YOU?

The most surprising thing about making a music video is how fun it can be, from production to the end product. It is so amazing to create something cool from nothing.

—Soo Wincci, Musician, Actress, Former Miss World Malaysia

This guide is written for the DIY crowd, with not a lot of money to spend and probably not a lot of experience with the ins and outs of music video creation. It will prepare you to get results that are as professional as possible—closer to MJ and further from early Bieber—without the accompanying budget. With the knowledge obtained from this book, you'll be well on your way to music video awesomeness!

ABOUT THE VIDEOS & COLOR PHOTOS

Many of the principles described in this book include short instructional videos to better explain and illustrate the concepts. Color photos of select images are also included to help you see the true depth of the pictures. To access the videos and photos, visit **www.halleonard.com/mylibrary** and enter the code found on page 1. From here you can download the photos and videos or stream/view them online. The videos and color photos are indicated with icons:

Video Icon   Photo Icon

Special thanks to video models Tom Scribner, Peter Scribner, Hannah Seaman, and Megan Seaman.

1.0: PRE-PRODUCTION

Planning your video

Pre-production, or the planning before you actually start filming, is an important part of creating an excellent music video.

IN MAKING A MUSIC VIDEO, I REALLY ENJOY FINDING THE CONCEPT OR STORY, AND ALL THE ARTISTIC CHOICES THAT SUPPORT THAT. BEING THE DIRECTOR OF A VIDEO FOR YOUR OWN MUSIC IS ALSO QUITE EMPOWERING, AS YOU AS THE SONGWRITER CAN EMPLOY A NEW MEDIUM TO HELP TELL OR ENHANCE THE STORY OF YOUR SONG.

–Shaudi Bianca Vahdat, American/Iranian Musician and Theatre Artist

For many DIYers, the pre-production phase might look like this:

You'll want to take it further than that, and this section will show you how. The better you plan, the better and smoother the rest of your music video production will be.

When we talk about pre-production, we'll go over four main areas:

1. **Your Vision:** Why are you making the video? What are your goals?
2. **Music Video Types:** What type of music video would best help you realize your vision?
3. **Planning** your DIY music video
4. **Choosing** a camera

The first part, vision, is something many DIYers wouldn't even think about. At least, it would seem obvious for most people: You want to make a music video so your song will surge in popularity. There are a few details to think about and plan so your end result will be something you're really happy with.

Next, we go over the three basic music video types, and the advantages and disadvantages of each. This section should help you consider some things you hadn't thought of before.

The planning chapter covers the nuts and bolts of the pre-production process. There are lots of elements, from large issues to small details, that deserve some thought. Of course, you can do minimal planning and just make it up as you go along, but that often turns out to be more work in the end. At a minimum, you'll want to take a little time for the different areas we discuss in this chapter.

> I'M ALWAYS SURPRISED AT HOW MUCH PLANNING GOES INTO MAKING A MUSIC VIDEO. FROM PRE-PRODUCTION AND PLANNING STAGES, ENDLESS REWRITES, AND MOST OF ALL TRYING TO COORDINATE SCHEDULES OF ACTORS AND ASSISTANTS, TIME SPENT PLANNING IS A NECESSARY EVIL THAT CAN GOBBLE UP TIME.
>
> *—Dav Abrams, Musician*

Finally, there's a special chapter on choosing a camera. The camera is one of the most important pieces of equipment for a music video, and there are lots of choices out there, so we'll look at what you might want and why.

1.1: WHAT'S YOUR VISION?

The GAT plan for music videos

With most music videos, the first thing you think about is the music: What song will you use as the audio track for your music video? It may be mixed and mastered already, or it may still be at the idea stage. Whatever the case, once you have some details about the "music" part of the music video, here's a simple way to start thinking about the "video" part.

> CREATING A VISION AND THEN MAKING IT REALITY THROUGH SHOOTING AND EDITING IS THE MOST ENJOYABLE PART ABOUT MAKING A MUSIC VIDEO.
>
> *—Naomi Westwater Weekes, Singer-Songwriter, Producer*

For the video side of your project, consider "G-A-T":

- Goals: What goals do you have for your music video? Why are you making it?
- Art: What artistic decisions will help you achieve your goals?
- Tech: What technical choices will help you create your art?

I use an illustration of a cat to help my students in their music video planning. In Valencian, the local language of the Spanish city where I teach, "gat" is the word for cat. The picture helps them keep Goals, Art, and Tech in the forefront of their minds.

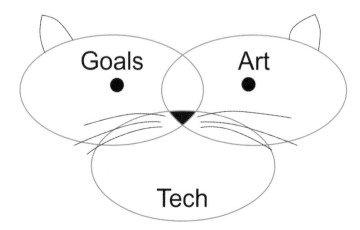

We'll cover planning the video in more detail in a later chapter, but for now, thinking about these three areas, in this order, can help focus your efforts to create a music video that does what you want it to do.

GOALS

THE HARDEST THING TO REMEMBER WHILE MAKING A MUSIC VIDEO
IS TO ALWAYS KEEP THE VERY FIRST OBJECTIVE YOU HAD, TO ALWAYS
FOCUS ON THE VERY FIRST IMAGES THAT CAME TO YOUR MIND
THE FIRST TIME YOU HEARD THE SONG. ALL THE THINGS THAT
CAME AFTER ARE LESS IMPORTANT THAN THAT.

–Greg et Lio, French Film Directors and Photographers

What would you like to accomplish with your music video? There are a variety of common reasons for creating a music video, particularly for the do-it-yourself video producer:

1. **Promote the artist.** Music videos can help sell more music, increase concert ticket sales, and just generally make the performer more popular. Promotion has always been the main reason most music videos are created.

REMEMBER THAT YOU HAVE A VOICE! IT'S IMPORTANT TO TRUST YOUR TEAM
AND LET PEOPLE DO THEIR WORK, BUT IF THE VIDEO IS FOR YOUR MUSIC,
IT'S PUBLICLY REPRESENTING YOU AS THE ARTIST AT THE END OF THE DAY,
AND IF SOMETHING DOESN'T FEEL RIGHT, IT'S YOUR RESPONSIBILITY
TO COMMUNICATE THAT TO THE DIRECTOR OR PRODUCER
(IN A RESPECTFUL AND KIND WAY, OF COURSE).

–Shaudi Bianca Vahdat, American/Iranian Musician and Theatre Artist

2. **Strengthen connections with the artist's audience**. A music video can make an artist more approachable to fans and help build strong relationships with them.

3. **Tell a good story.** You may want to create a narrative video, either to reinforce the story being told by the music, or to tell an entirely different story.

4. **Express your artistic vision.** Music videos are a great vehicle for expressing creativity, since they can combine sounds and images in almost unlimited combinations, unconstrained by the conventions of many other types of movies and videos.

MAKING A MUSIC VIDEO IS FUN AND INTUITIVE. IT'S NOT THAT DIFFERENT
FROM MAKING MUSIC—EVEN DOWN TO THE SOFTWARE. I SUGGEST PEOPLE
TRY TO MAKE VIDEOS THEMSELVES IF THEY CAN. THAT WAY,
THE VIDEO CAN BE AN EXTENSION OF THE SONG.

–Laser Malena-Webber, Musician, Music Video Director

5. **Learn something.** Making a music video will help you learn lots of interesting skills, and for do-it-yourself producers, this can be a legitimate goal. For example, are you interested in stop-motion animation? Creating a stop-motion music video is one of the best ways to learn by doing.

ART

WHEN THE AUDIENCE AND ARTIST LIKE THE VIDEO,
ALL THE HARD WORK IS WORTH IT. IT IS AN ART FORM WHERE
YOU PARTICIPATE IN PRODUCING THE IMAGE OF THE MUSIC.

–Simon Yu, Musician, Music Video Director

Once you've defined your goals, you're ready to consider the "art" part, the artistic choices that will support your goals. Typically, the artistic vision comes from a collaboration between the director and the performers, although it could be mostly or entirely one or the other. The artistic choices will include things like the type of music video, the cast, the location and setting, and the look and feel.

Music

At the center of any music video is the music. If it's your song and your recording, you probably know it backward and forward. If you are working on a video for someone else, you'll want to get familiar with the music and the performers. Listen to the song many times. Talk with the performers about what ideas they have, what moods they want to create, what stories are in the song or are connected with the song.

> A MUSIC VIDEO IS ONLY AS GOOD AS THE SONG. YOU'VE GOT TO OBJECTIVELY TAKE A STEP BACK AND RECOGNIZE THAT.
>
> *—Oliver Kersey, British Singer-Songwriter*

Type of Music Video

What type of music video will you make? You will usually decide on a performance video, a narrative (telling a story), or a conceptual video (for more abstract creations), although you could combine different types. We'll talk about these in more detail in the next chapter.

Cast

Who will be in your music video? If you're making a performance video, your cast will usually include the performers, but there may be others as well—dancers, cameos, or anonymous crowds. Make up your wish list here. In the planning stage you'll see what's practical, and get specific commitments from people.

Location and Setting

Where will your music video take place? The location and setting could be a plain, featureless room or an exotic location halfway around the world. It will probably require physical access, although it may (also or instead) be created digitally. You won't make definite arrangements until the planning stage later on, but starting to think about location and setting now will help shape your ideas about your video.

Look and Feel

This is where you plan in general terms what the video will look like—what sort of vibe or mood it will have. You might think about colors, sets, lighting, time of day, costumes, and other aspects you can specify in detail in your music video plan.

> THE BIGGEST THING I LEARNED FROM MAKING/BEING IN A MUSIC VIDEO IS BEING CLEAR WITH YOUR IDEA, HAVING SAMPLE VIDEOS FOR THE DIRECTOR OR VIDEOGRAPHER, SO THEY UNDERSTAND THE VIBE YOU'RE CREATING.
>
> *—Naomi Westwater Weekes, Singer-Songwriter, Producer*

TECH

For music videos especially, good art requires good tech: not necessarily the most expensive equipment, but the right equipment (or a reasonable DIY equivalent) and the skill to use it properly. The tech is what you need to bring your artistic vision to life.

For most performers, this may be the least interesting part of the project: they'll care more about the final result than about how that result is achieved. If you are an artist creating your own video, this may be an area where you will need to build some expertise as well as look for help from those who already have the skills you need.

Although some videos can be produced using only a computer, in most cases, your tech begins with a camera (plus batteries, media storage cards, etc.), and may include stabilizers, lights, and a variety of other gear, as well as editing software. We'll go more in depth about gear in the planning chapter.

VISION AT A GLANCE

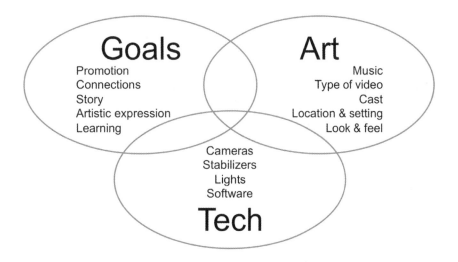

Goals

- Promote the artist
- Strengthen connections with the artist's audience
- Tell a good story
- Express your artistic vision
- Learn something

Art

- Music
- Type of music video
- Cast
- Location and setting
- Look and feel

Tech

- Cameras
- Stabilizers
- Lights
- Software

NEXT STEPS

Having considered and outlined a general idea of the Goals, Art, and Tech for your music video, you're ready to create a more detailed plan. Careful planning almost always means a better music video, involving less expense and less hassle than if you skip the planning stage.

Since one of the first steps of a good plan is deciding the type of music video you want to make, let's look deeper into the three main types of music videos, what they do best, and why you might want to choose one type over the others.

1.2: MUSIC VIDEO TYPES

Three main types of music videos, and why you would choose each one

You might think that because the medium of music video allows artists almost total artistic freedom, it would be hard to sort music videos into meaningful categories. Surprising as it is, most music videos can be grouped into one of three types: **performance**, **narrative**, and **conceptual**.

A single music video can have aspects of two or even all three types (for example, a music video can both show a performance and tell a story), but one of the types usually stands out. Understanding the advantages and challenges of the different types of music videos can help as you think about the music video you want to make.

PERFORMANCE MUSIC VIDEOS

Performance music videos are the most common—which makes sense, since the purpose of a music video is usually to promote a performer or group, and often the easiest and most effective way to do that is to feature them in a performance video.

The main advantage of performance videos is that they usually provide a natural and effective way to showcase the performer. This kind of video helps forge a connection between the performer and the audience, as happens in a live performance.

> THE MOST ENJOYABLE PART ABOUT MAKING A MUSIC VIDEO IS A TIE BETWEEN
> 1. WATCHING A FANTASTIC PERFORMER ABSOLUTELY
> LIGHT UP THE CAMERA OVER AND OVER AGAIN, AND
> 2. REALIZING THIS IS ONE OF THOSE PROJECTS EVERYONE IS DOING
> BECAUSE THEY REALLY CARE, AND IT STOPS BEING "WORK."
>
> *—Nick Clark, Film Producer, Director and Editor*

Also, live or studio performance videos can be the easiest to film and edit, since they merely follow the plan of the musical performance itself. The video crew is mainly there to record the experience.

Planning a performance video may be comparatively simple, but because this type of video is so common, it's not easy to create a work that will stand out from the crowd. Another challenge is that the video director usually has little control over the performance, so she has to capture what she can while keeping out of the way of the main event.

Studio Recordings

Performance videos at their most basic involve setting up video recording equipment to capture the performance of the song. This could be a live performance in a concert or other setting, or a recording of the song in a studio. Studio recordings are often the easiest to record, although they do have some challenges.

The main point of a studio performance is to produce the music for a professionally mixed and mastered recording. Although the audio is recorded at the same time, it's typically handled separately by a different team, and the video director's job is to record the experience as it happens for sharing with a larger audience later.

In a studio, time usually costs money, so you may not have the luxury of repeating the entire song or parts of it just for the sake of the video. Even so, you can make the most of shooting video in a studio by

- Having multiple cameras recording from different angles, including overhead, from the side, or even mounted on instruments using small action cameras
- Setting the lighting carefully before the recording starts, to get the best possible lighting conditions and to control the mood of the video
- Suggesting different visual treatments (in addition to lighting, these can include coordinated costumes, props, backdrops, etc.) whose main purpose is to enhance the video.

With studio recordings, there are always multiple takes of the audio, which give an opportunity for different video shots, although the nature of the takes varies depending on the type of music being produced.

For music recorded to a click track or metronome, not only can multiple sessions be mixed for audio recording (recording the vocalist separate from the drummer, for instance), but multiple video recordings of the different sessions can be mixed together as well.

As long as the video equipment doesn't get in the way of the recording engineers, different takes provide the opportunity to change camera angles and positions, adjust lighting, or otherwise vary the visuals to make a more interesting video mix in the end.

There are some studio recordings (think jazz and classical music) that aren't recorded to a metronome and may even be significantly different from one take to the next. You don't have the option of mixing and matching different shots from different takes—if you try, you may run into serious synchronization and other audio/video matching issues.

In these cases, you can set up multiple cameras to record each take, keeping track of the different takes on the different cameras, so when the final audio recording is chosen, you can have the corresponding shots from several cameras to work with.

Live Performances

Live performances are similar to studio recordings in that the main reason for the activity is not to get the video—you're just there to record what happens, although in interesting ways that will look great afterwards.

The main differences are (1) you only get one chance to record, since the band isn't going to repeat the song if your camera is out of focus or your memory card is full, and (2) you have to make sure you don't detract from the show by getting in the way of the audience, or sometimes even being visible on or near the stage.

Visibility for the video recording can be an extra challenge, since lighting that may look great in a live performance may be hard to capture properly on video—lots of dark areas contrasted with extremely bright spots, flashing colored lights, and more. Try to work with the lighting crew ahead of time to find lighting that will meet both your needs, or at least try to film the dress rehearsal or lighting check so you can figure out what setup will help you get the best possible exposure during the concert.

Even more important than with studio recordings, you'll want to have multiple cameras so you can get as many angles as possible for any given song. Unobtrusive action cams deliberately placed around the stage can be a big help. Also, make sure you have the free memory and batteries you need to record the entire performance, including extras in case something goes wrong. You get one chance, and if your battery dies or your card fills up during a number, that chance is gone.

I wish I had an SD card for every time a student of mine has started recording a music video, only to find out that they forgot to clear off the pictures on their memory card from their weekend trip to Mallorca or some other exotic place, so they run out of space before the song is over. Or the battery has died before the filming is over, and they don't have any extras.

Scripted Performances

Besides concerts and studio sessions, performance music videos also include *scripted* performances. In this type of video, the main point is still to highlight the performer, but creating the video is the main goal, not just a secondary concern, so the artistic control is in the hands of the video director. For a scripted performance, the audio has usually been mixed and mastered ahead of time; the performer's main job, besides any acting required, is to sing and play along with the recording, convincingly and perfectly in sync.

Most big-budget mainstream performance videos are scripted. They focus on the musicians and their performance, but they take place in a variety of exotic, unusual, or completely computer-generated environments.

Sometimes the video also features a strong storyline (as in many of Taylor Swift's videos), so the video is as much narrative as it is performance. At other times, the video has an overriding theme or gimmick (think of OK Go's videos), so it is really a conceptual/performance hybrid.

NARRATIVE MUSIC VIDEOS

Narrative videos are videos that tell a story. Popular songs often tell a story, so a narrative video is a natural fit for those types of songs. But a narrative video can be a good choice for any type of music video, because (well-told) stories are naturally so engaging.

> THE BIGGEST THING I LEARNED FROM MAKING AND BEING IN A MUSIC VIDEO IS THAT IT'S ALL ABOUT STORYTELLING, AND MORE = LESS.
>
> *—Dav Abrams, Musician*

We humans have been telling stories for thousands of years, and we continue to like them because they work: the story moves along from one scene to another, there's a conflict that needs to be resolved, and the story elements compel the audience to stay to hear what happens next. Nearly all books, movies, plays, and other shows follow a narrative arc—we find them compelling and they are more likely to appeal to a large audience.

> REMEMBER YOU ARE TELLING A STORY, AND SIMPLY USING YOUR FILMMAKING TOOLS TO TELL IT. IT CAN BE DIFFICULT TO REMEMBER THIS WHEN YOUR EQUIPMENT IS NOT WHAT YOU WISH IT WERE, OR WHEN THE SHOTS LOOK BEAUTIFUL BUT DON'T ADD TO THE SONG. EVEN IF IT'S JUST PERFORMANCE SHOTS, IT'S A STORY. MAKE IT AN INTERESTING ONE WITH WHAT YOU HAVE!
>
> *—Anjie Concepcion, Audio-Visual Artist, Songwriter, Music Video Director*

Of course, entire books and university courses have been written about how to create a good story, so that won't be covered here. It's worth noting, though, that while we all have experience hearing and telling stories, creating a good story can be a challenge. Even multi-million-dollar movie blockbusters (or blockbuster wannabees) can fall short in creating a good story, despite plenty of effort.

On the DIY side, a few years ago some students of mine put together a narrative video that had lots of great things going for it—a powerful original song, beautiful cinematography, interesting characters, nice lighting—but the story wasn't as clear as the creators intended. I sometimes use the video as an example in my class because most people who see the video miss that it's a story of love gone wrong. What the creators thought was obvious was just too subtle. A couple of crucial elements, an engagement ring and some poison, are too small on screen and go by too quickly. This failure teaches the importance of testing your story with people unconnected with its creation to see if they can understand what is going on.

Types of Narratives

The structure of a narrative music video follows the structure of the story. These stories can take inspiration and form from existing stories, and there are lots of options for structure—not just starting with "once upon a time" and ending with "and they all lived happily ever after."

We won't cover all the options for creating narratives, but keep in mind the following possibilities, in addition to starting at the beginning of the story and going to the end:

- Showing the end, or just before the end, then going back to the beginning to show how the end came about.
- Starting at the middle and repeatedly returning to earlier points via flashbacks. Gwen Stefani's "Cool" is a good example.
- Presenting two or more parallel narratives that come together at the end—or not.
- Starting at the end and going back to the beginning in reverse narrative order. The video for "The Scientist" by Coldplay takes it a step further and actually records the song in reverse.

More complicated narratives require more effort to produce successfully, particularly given the potential confusion they could cause if not done well, and the limited time (typically less than three or four minutes) available in a music video. Still, they can be very creative and a lot of fun to produce.

Types of Narrative Videos

The video narrative can follow the story of the song, if there is one, or it can tell a story indirectly related to the song, or it can present a story that has nothing to do with the song, making the music like an unrelated soundtrack.

Videos for Story Songs

Because songs so often tell stories, the music video script can almost write itself, and filming is a matter of creating video images to reinforce the narrative. With the storyline already developed, you can concentrate your attention on other artistic choices such as the mood, the setting, and the physical appearance of the characters in the story, like Taylor Swift does in "Blank Space."

Somewhat-Related Story Videos

Some songs hint at a story, or they talk about a general situation, and the music video takes that situation and develops it into a story with a strong narrative. Sia's "Cheap Thrills" is a good example; the song talks about having fun inexpensively at a dance, and the video presents a 1950s TV-special dance contest with some unexpected contestants.

Unrelated Story Videos

Some songs may not tell a strong story – they may even be entirely instrumental or abstract – but they can still be used for narrative videos. Also, a song may tell one story while the video tells another.

The music video for "Radioactive" by Imagine Dragons presents a clear story that, as far as I can tell, has nothing to do with the song. The story of the song is open to interpretation, but it's unlikely that a listener would think the song is about stuffed animals battling in a run-down barn-turned-betting-parlor. And yet the video presents a clear narrative (introduction, action, climax, resolution), and is a good example of how creative storytelling can be used in any situation.

CONCEPTUAL MUSIC VIDEOS

A conceptual music video is centered on a particular concept, artistic or otherwise, rather than primarily showing a performance or telling a story. A conceptual video often focuses on the visuals, making them as compelling and interesting as possible, setting a certain mood as defined by the artistic vision of the creator.

> CONTINUITY IS THE MOST IMPORTANT THING IN VIDEO. THIS IS FAIRLY "EASY" WITH A NARRATIVE PIECE, AS THE STORY/DIALOGUE MAKES A CLEAR THREAD TO FOLLOW, BUT ABSTRACT VISUALS ARE NOT AS EASY, AND IN MANY STUDENT WORKS I SEE CONTINUITY IS EASILY FORGOTTEN. THIS MIGHT BE THE NUMBER-ONE ISSUE WITH YOUR FIRST FILM.
>
> *—Pierce Warnecke, Sound and Video Artist and Educator*

Conceptual videos could include the following:

- Dance videos (where the dancers are not those performing the music)
- Videos with abstract images
- Videos of images connected by a theme (which may be the song or something else)
- Videos that focus on a particular technique, such as projection mapping, stop-motion animation (if it is not telling a story), and so forth
- Lyric videos

The music videos for "Katachi" by Shugo Tokumaru (PVC stop-motion animations by Kijek/Adamski) and "Resynthesis" by Max Cooper (video animations by Kevin McGloughlin) are fascinating examples of exploring different artistic concepts and techniques in a video.

Conceptual videos can be great on their own, but interesting concepts can also be added to and intertwined with performance or narrative videos to make the overall production more creative and engaging. Jain's "Come" music video is clearly a performance, but the video also explores the concept of interesting visual tricks and special effects throughout the song.

COMPARING THE THREE TYPES OF MUSIC VIDEOS

Type	Options	Structure	Pros	Cons
Performance	• Studio, click track, many takes • Concert • Lip sync to mixed track • Combination of above • Studio, multi-camera, one take	Follow performance from beginning to end	• Get to see and know performer • Promote performer • Personal connection • Great if viewer knows and likes the performer	• Most common • Harder to make outstanding
Narrative	• Follow story of song • Story but not directly related to song • Not a traditional narrative but with a narrative arc: A B C	Dictated by narrative, but doesn't have to be linear	• We are naturally attracted • By definition and design, they make us want to stay • Can take inspiration and form from existing stories • Lots of options for structure	• Needs more formal structure that makes sense as a story • Needs more careful planning
Conceptual	• Include performer, but no performance • Connect to song but no performer • Unrelated images & actions • Abstract images	Completely open; can be structured around performance or not, or a narrative or not	• Unlimited creativity	• Unlimited creativity • Easier to lose audience

If you consider the three main stages of video production—planning, filming, and editing (also known as pre-production, production, and post-production)—different music video types require different levels of effort at each stage.

For performance music videos, the performers are obviously the key, so you want them to look their best. This takes pre-production planning, but the emphasis will be on the filming, especially for a live performance or studio recording, since the main point of the activity is not the video but the performance or recording.

A good narrative video requires more pre-production planning than a performance video. You want to put as much effort as possible into creating a compelling story and planning how it will be filmed. Once the cameras start to roll, if you don't have a good story, it's unlikely that it will get better from that point on.

The process for making a conceptual video might involve a lot of pre-production work (developing a concept that will be worth your time and effort), but sometimes very little planning goes into it, and most of the work happens in post-production, since these types of videos often rely on post special effects and other complicated editing.

MUSIC VIDEO TYPES AT A GLANCE

Performance music videos

- Studio recordings
- Live performances
- Scripted performances

Narrative music videos

- Videos for story songs
- Somewhat related story videos
- Unrelated story videos

Conceptual music videos

- Dance
- Abstract images
- Thematic images
- Technique
- Lyrics

1.3: PLANNING YOUR MUSIC VIDEO

With your vision statement, you've covered the *why* of the video, and a little of the *what*. In the planning stage, you put together the details of what you'll be doing, as well as who, when, where, and how.

While big-budget videos have elaborate plans, you may have a very simple music video idea—for example, you'll be playing at a concert, and someone will be there to film it. But even with the simplest ideas, it's helpful to go over the planning steps to see if there's anything you might have overlooked. More preparation usually makes for a better video.

MAKE SURE YOU ARE HAPPY WITH YOUR VIDEO'S CONCEPT AND DECIDE ON HOW YOU'RE GOING TO EXECUTE THE CONCEPT. PLANNING IS EVERYTHING. WHAT EQUIPMENT DO I NEED? WHERE AM I SHOOTING? DO I NEED PERMISSION TO SHOOT THERE? DO I NEED AN EXTRA HAND TO SHOOT? DO I NEED PEOPLE TO ACT IN THIS VIDEO? HOW LONG DO I NEED TO SHOOT? YOU WILL ALWAYS UNDERESTIMATE THIS. GIVE YOURSELF TIME.

—Steve Umculo, South African Musician and Entertainer

In this section, we'll look at the following areas:

- The planning cycles
- Treatments and other descriptions of what happens in the video
- Locations
- Budget
- Cast
- Equipment
- Art and effects
- Crew
- Schedule and logistics

THE MOST ENJOYABLE PART ABOUT MAKING A MUSIC VIDEO IS IN THE PRE-PRODUCTION STAGES, WHEN EVERYONE IS SPITBALLING IDEAS AND DREAMING BIG. EVENTUALLY REALITY SETS IN AND YOU END UP SETTLING FOR WHAT IS REALISTICALLY POSSIBLE WITH YOUR SCHEDULE/BUDGET/TECHNOLOGY CAPABILITY/AVAILABILITY OF ACTORS/ETC., BUT FOR THAT SHORT WHILE THE SKY'S THE LIMIT AND YOUR VIDEO IS GOING TO CANNES.

–Dav Abrams, Musician

THE PLANNING CYCLES

As is the case with any complicated project, successful planning doesn't just happen once in a single sitting. For everything to go smoothly, you're likely to go around and around on the same topics. We've already started the planning process with the GAT plan, but we'll look at some of those same areas again in more detail. Once you have a good treatment (described below), you may refine your descriptions further with storyboards and shot lists. At some point, you may realize you don't have the equipment for what you originally envisioned, or part of your great idea is completely impractical, so you will have to come back to your original idea and make some modifications.

When you finally get your footage, you will probably come around again, since you may have some scenes that didn't turn out the way you expected, or you may have other great scenes you didn't expect at all. In the editing process, you will refine things even further.

This isn't a bad thing: it's the way the creative process works. As you gain experience, there will be less variation between the original idea and final product, but part of the fun of the process is seeing what your idea becomes as you move through each stage of creation.

I'M ALWAYS SURPRISED AT THE END PRODUCT. IT ALWAYS TURNS OUT DIFFERENT THAN YOU INITIALLY EXPECTED. PROVIDED YOU WORK WITH THE RIGHT PEOPLE, IT'S BETTER THAN EXPECTED.

–Oliver Kersey, British Singer-Songwriter

The same goes for other areas of the planning process. For instance, with locations, you first get an idea. Then you go to check out the location. Later you check with the owners or others who can give permissions and permits, if needed. On the day of filming, you need to make sure everyone and everything gets to where they need to be.

Lighting is another example: We talk about it briefly in this chapter, then go into much more detail in two chapters in the Production section. It's an area you'll keep cycling back to. Lighting planning starts with considering what mood you want to create, where you will be shooting and what time of day, but comes around again with what lighting equipment you will need, then what equipment you can actually get, then on to learning how to use it, safely transporting it to the location, getting everything powered and turned on and positioned, and so on.

You can't really check "lights" off your list until you've dealt with the lights at each of these stages. "We'll see when we get there" and "I'm sure it will work out fine" are the sorts of phrases that are most likely to come back to bite you. Yes, there's plenty of room for spontaneity in music video making, but you can get the most out of that spontaneity only after your planning and preparation have created the well-oiled production machine that can support it.

DESCRIBE WHAT HAPPENS: TREATMENTS AND MORE

The description of what happens in the music video is typically called a "treatment." It can be a simple explanation of the idea, or a detailed, scene-by-scene narrative, complete with drawings and photographs.

The treatment should describe the music video in enough detail that every key decision maker—director, producer, performers—can read it and have a similar vision and idea of what happens in the video and what it's about. If you put together a solid treatment and get buy-in from all the relevant parties, the rest of the process will go much more smoothly.

If your video concept is straightforward, a few sentences or paragraphs describing what will happen may suffice. If you have more involved ideas, this might be where you want to put together a script, storyboards, and/or a shot list.

Scripts and beat sheets

Once you have a treatment, another round in the video description planning cycle might be to create a script and/or a beat sheet. A script has a story written out in detail, while a beat sheet gives only the main highlights as bullet points, typically for each new scene or when something new happens. These are most important if you're telling a story with a narrative video, since in good stories things happen in a certain order, and it's hard to make them up in the moment.

Storyboards

A storyboard is a further refinement in the description process, helping you visualize the scenes you want to create and saving time when you are filming. A storyboard is like a cartoon or graphic novel (although the drawings don't have to be more than geometric shapes and stick figures), with a rectangle showing just the major scenes or every significant change that happens in the video, along with a brief description (which could be from the beat sheet). Creating a storyboard requires you to be able to anticipate what you want the camera to see when you film, since you are roughly creating the camera's viewfinder before it happens.

> PLANNING AHEAD AND CREATING THE STORYBOARD IS THE MOST IMPORTANT THING FOR MAKING A MUSIC VIDEO. IT IS SO HARD TO CAPTURE THE CORRECT FOOTAGE WHEN I HAVEN'T ALREADY DECIDED WHAT SHOTS I NEED BEFORE FILMING. WITHOUT A CLEAR ROADMAP, IT IS DIFFICULT TO HAPPEN UPON A DESTINATION.
>
> *—Savannah Philyaw, Indie-Folk Singer-Songwriter*

If you haven't done this before, it can be a little daunting—you may not really know what you want everything to look like before you film. Storyboarding is a learned skill, so don't worry if it doesn't come together right away. Giving it a try can help you clarify your thinking, even if it doesn't result in a detailed roadmap for filming.

Shot lists

A shot list is another way of describing your video, listing every shot you need to take. It is particularly useful during production, because shot lists are arranged by location or setting rather than by the sequence of scenes in the final video, making your shooting schedule much more efficient and organized. For example, if you are filming a narrative music video, and something happens in a café at the beginning and the end of the video, you'll generally want to shoot both café shots during the same setup to save time. A shot list will help you plan for it.

There are various tables and spreadsheets available online to use as a template, but you can easily make your own. A good shot list will include the location or setting, who is in the shot, the type of shot and camera movement (which we talk about in a later chapter), the main events that happen, and the main objects in the shot.

In some cases, a shot list might not be necessary, particularly for a non-narrative music video. You could shoot the entire song a few times in one location or with one setup, then change and shoot it again, going all the way through the song each time. The decision of which shot goes where in the final video happens when you are editing and can see what looks best for each part of the song.

LOCATIONS

For the locations that will appear in your video, be as specific and as prepared as possible. For a low-key DIY music video, you won't need as much preparation as for a large-scale production with a large crew and lots of equipment (and liability), but more preparation will help you avoid problems. It's hard to make a video if your location plans fall through.

Some of my students were filming a music video in a low-key Mexican restaurant, which was the perfect setting for the song. They weren't even playing music or causing a ruckus, and I think they were the only ones in the restaurant, but as soon as the owner saw them, he kicked them out, saying they couldn't film there. Be sure to ask first.

Location scouting

Once you have the initial idea of where you want to make your music video, visit the location and see if it lives up to what you imagined in your head. You may remember it incorrectly, or you may never have been there and just thought it would work.

For a low-budget DIY production, you probably won't be able to travel across oceans or continents to get to the ideal spot, so choose a location you can travel to easily to check it out. If it is too far to travel to except on the day of the shoot, do as much research as you can through pictures and contacts who are local to the area.

For any visits, go at the time of day you plan to shoot—and if appropriate, the time of year. (If you are planning a midsummer shoot, visiting the area when it's buried in snow will be less useful.)

In your initial visits, here are some things you should make a note of to ensure a successful outcome:

- **Lighting:** What will the lighting be like (sun, streetlights, overhead lights, etc.)? Will you be able to control the lighting? If you want it completely dark (so you can use your own lights), will that be possible?

- **Safety and security**: Will the safety of equipment and the crew be an issue? Is there a place to store your gear safely?

- **Noise:** Is there noise from crowds, traffic, etc.? Will you have a problem hearing your recording if you are lip-synching? Will your music bother others?

- **Transportation**: How will you transport people and gear to the site? Is there adequate parking? Will it be difficult to haul gear from vehicles to the final filming site?

- **Other people:** Are there likely to be other people there when you are shooting? Will that cause a problem? Are strangers likely to wander into your shots? (You may need to get written permission from anyone who is identifiable in the video.)

- **Power:** If you will need access to electricity, is it likely to be available?
- **Environment:** Will there be a problem with water, dirt, wind, or anything else that could affect people or equipment? If outside, what is the weather likely to be?
- **Existing setup:** Will you have adequate space for what you plan to do? Will be you able to get the camera far enough away from the scene for the shots you want to take? Are there distracting things that will be in the background of shots? Can you move things out of the way if you need to?

Scheduling and permissions

When you are confident your location will work for your needs, make sure you can use it when you want it. A small DIY crew can be more flexible and less noticeable than a large professional project, but most places, public or private, are likely to require permission and may require scheduling to make sure it will be available when it is needed. You may also need insurance or permits for your planned location, and maybe even a police presence (which probably would knock out most DIY budgets).

A former student of mine had a great idea for a music video in a private tourist attraction in Barcelona. He worked out the scheduling and had the budget for the usage fee. Everything seemed to be going fine until he found he also needed a million dollars' worth of liability insurance, even though it was just him and his friend with a camera and a tripod for a couple of hours of shooting. He decided to go somewhere else.

When inquiring about public spaces, it may take a lot of asking around until you find the person who can give permission. Do as much checking ahead of time as you can, since the rules and attitudes in some locations are much more hostile to DIY filming than in others.

Confirming location details

For another round in the location cycle, if you've scheduled a place, it's a good idea to confirm a few days ahead that everything will be ready when the time arrives. If you've arranged for power, transportation, security, or anything else, makes sure all the loose ends are tied up so you won't have surprises on the day of filming that will mess up your plans.

BUDGET

You may be thinking, "What do you mean, budget?" You might hope that you could make your video with a budget of zero, but some parts of the process will go much better if you can come up with a little cash.

THE HARDEST THING ABOUT MAKING A MUSIC VIDEO IS THAT IT IS USUALLY A RUN AGAINST TIME OR RESOURCES. THESE LIMITING FACTORS CAN LEAD TO CREATIVE SOLUTIONS AND THEY USUALLY DO, BUT IT IS JUST AS COMMON TO COME UP WITH AN IDEA WHICH IS IMPOSSIBLE TO EXECUTE WITHIN YOUR GIVEN MEANS.

- Kasia Kijek and Przemek Adamski, Polish Film Directors and Animators

On the very low end of budgeting, where you've been able to borrow a camera and have your friends volunteer their time to help out, plan to budget for snacks and drinks, or to buy your crew a meal if they're on the job for a long time.

At the other end of the DIY scale, you might be budgeting for renting or buying equipment and for hiring some professional crew (at least a director and a camera operator), and you could have expenses connected to locations, transportation, cast, etc.

You can approach the budget in a couple of ways. One is to have some money set aside, then go through the rest of the planning process below and figure out where you want to spend it to get the biggest bang for your buck. Another is to go through the planning and figure out everything you can beg for or borrow, then come up with money for the rest in another phase of the budget cycle. That may be through finding relatives who want to support a good cause, or setting up a campaign on an online donation site.

CAST

The cast is everyone who appears in the video. It may be no one, it may be just band members, or it may include dancers or sword swallowers or mongrel hordes.

Planning for your cast will also go through various cycles. First, imagine who or what types of people (such as skateboarders or cliff divers) you might want in the video. You can be as ambitious as you like, realizing that some people won't be able to be in your video for a variety of reasons.

Next, track them down and ask if they'd like to be in your production. You may have decided to budget some money to hire professionals, or you may be looking strictly for volunteers. Be prepared to have those conversations, including why your volunteers will have such a great time being a part of your cast.

Once you also have a crew (discussed below), find a time to film that will meet everyone's schedule. The more people you have, the harder this will be, but using online calendars and scheduling tools can be a huge help with this task. It's important at this point to make sure you have contact information for everyone, in case someone gets lost on the day of filming. (I've seen it happen.)

Finally, consider whether you need written permission from everyone in the cast to appear in the video. Your legal team, if you had one, would say "yes" in every case. If it's just the band and you're all in it together, maybe not. If it's just your friends... you decide, but it can't hurt, and adds a measure of seriousness to your project. (Check out wonder.legal "model release forms" online for some great free, customizable forms.)

EQUIPMENT

After you plan the where and the who, you can work on exactly what equipment you need to make your vision a reality. Here are the main things to consider:

Camera(s)

Of course, your camera or cameras are usually the most important piece of equipment. Choosing a camera is a little complicated, so the entire next chapter is dedicated to that question.

Having more than one camera, if you can, is nearly always a good idea, for different angles of the same shot or for backup if one camera dies, etc. A student of mine was filming a school performance with three different cameras, each pointing at the stage from a different angle. Since the performance was probably going to be longer than the battery life of any give camera (it was), she was prepared with spare batteries to swap into the cameras on a staggered schedule so there were always at least two cameras filming at any given time.

Batteries

Batteries aren't primary gear, but they deserve a special mention, since generally the camera and other equipment such as lights need batteries to operate. If your batteries die and you don't have any spares, then the shoot is over, regardless of what else is in place. As Steve Umculo, musician and former student says:

When making a music video, always remember to charge the damn batteries! I can't tell you how many times this has hindered me. Only have one? buy more! and charge them!

Storage media

The storage media is your "film": SD cards, or whatever media your camera uses, as well as external hard disks or thumb drives for backing up the files. Without the files, there is no video, so keep close track of your storage media. However small your DIY budget is, you will need some cash for storage media, including extras for shooting and space for backups. Don't skimp on this one. Also, put labels on your SD cards so you can tell them apart.

Tripods and other supports

In most cases, you'll want a tripod, or at least a reliable way to support the camera in a fixed position. Someone you know probably has a tripod.

Tripods (and tripod heads, which are always separate on more expensive setups) can cost anywhere from a few bucks to more than your used car. The more expensive ones are sturdier (and heavier), and more expensive tripod heads are more secure and allow for smoother movement, especially with large professional cameras.

You may be able to get by with a semi-cheap tripod, since it will probably hold your camera in one place. But if you want to do any pans or tilts with the tripod, a good tripod head will give you much better results. More expensive tripods will also hold together longer, since the cheaper ones come with a lot of little plastic parts that are likely to break. If you treat them carefully, they can last a long time, and they can work for holding up smaller cameras or even lights in an emergency. Just make sure your camera is securely attached and the legs are securely locked in place, so nothing falls over or falls off.

If you want the smooth movements that are easiest with a pro tripod, you can usually obtain one from a camera rental business on a daily or weekly basis for not too much money.

Lighting gear

After the camera/tripod, lighting is usually the next most important equipment for a professional-looking video. We talk all about lighting in the Production section, so plan to read that as part of your ongoing planning about lighting.

Lighting gear may include battery- or AC-powered lights, light stands, covers, reflectors, shades, colored filters, and more. If you're filming outside in sunlight, you may not need anything else, but almost every other situation will benefit from extra lighting.

If you haven't made an investment in camera lighting gear (or don't have a friend who has), try gathering together whatever lamps and shop lights you have around. Given the importance of lighting, this is a place where spending money to rent at least some equipment will make a big difference in your final product.

Movement gear

These are camera stabilizers (such as Steadicam™), including motorized gimbals, dollies (carts with wheels, sometimes on special tracks), and other equipment to help get smooth, stable moving camera shots.

In the Production section of this book, there's an entire chapter on camera movement. We consider the issue here because if you want a lot of movement for the video, you may need to rent specialized equipment. Think about the types of shots you want and what you might need to get them, and read the movement chapter for more ideas.

Audio gear

In most cases, the audio creation is separate from the music video production. Because music videos deal with musicians who have previously created and produced their music track, audio needs for music videos should be very basic. Either you'll be lip-synching to a pre-recorded track, or, in a studio or live concert, you'll have a separate sound crew with equipment dedicated to getting the audio you need for an audio recording as well as for the video.

If you plan to lip-sync, it's important to play the pre-recorded track loudly enough for the performers to play or sing along with it. A phone with the track and a decent bluetooth speaker will often do the job, but test it first. If the playing devices (phone and speaker) need to run off a battery, make sure they are fully charged.

Computer (and software)

A computer's primary role is at the editing stage, using the appropriate software of your choice. Editing is one of the most resource-intensive activities a computer can do, so a top-of-the-line processor and lots of RAM and hard disk space will make your life much easier.

Also, having a laptop along during production will allow you to review footage on the set to make sure you are getting the recordings you expect. It's one more (expensive) piece of gear to keep track of, but it can be very handy.

The equipment planning cycles

Equipment can be complicated because there can be so much of it, sometimes coming from different places, and probably all worth a lot of money. As with other aspects of preparation, first plan on what you want, then see what you can get and afford. A third round of the cycle is making the arrangements to get it all, a fourth is actually picking it up and getting it to your location. You could also include here learning how to use unfamiliar equipment, including downloading a copy of the user manual.

The equipment must then be set up. Remember to schedule adequate time and have enough crew on site to do it. Even a few cameras, tripods, light stands, and lights can take a surprisingly long time to set up and get positioned properly, especially if you or your team are inexperienced. Add to that the possibility (which happens frequently) that you might get all set up and then decide the look just isn't right. You need to try a different corner of the room or go around the corner to see if that works better, moving gear and positioning it all over again.

After you have used it, you need to put it all away, making sure all the little bits get in the right bags (and there are often lots of little bits). Finally, you need to get it back safely to where it belongs.

The more gear you get, the better it is to keep a written record of what you have so you can keep track of it and make sure your uncle gets his prized camera (with all the lens caps) back when you're all done.

ART AND EFFECTS

This isn't equipment, but it's more "stuff" you may need to gather for your video shoot. For a low/no-budget shoot, these small extra touches can make a big difference, and a little creativity can go a long way.

Costumes

You may not need anything special that isn't already in the band members' closets, but it's a good idea to give some thought to what the band and cast members will wear. A certain type of clothing or certain colors might help your DIY video stand out—even a simple guideline like "everyone wear blue jeans and dark shirts." With luck, you'll know a theater buff who is good with this sort of thing and who can apply their creativity to your project.

Also, in case your video makes it big, it's best to avoid shirts with logos or other trademarked images. You don't want to have to haggle with anybody's lawyers over what's on your shirt.

Hair and makeup

Fixing your hair and makeup might be part of your daily routine, or it might be something you have never thought about, but a professional production always pays attention to it. Even the most basic DIY project should avoid hair that's sticking up in a distracting way (unless that's your look), and a little powder can keep your forehead from shining like a light bulb. If makeup isn't your thing, perhaps you can find that friend who loves doing this and can recommend the sprays and gels and whatever else you will need.

Props

If you're doing a narrative or concept video, you may need some props. For example, a project in one of my classes took the "Little Red Riding Hood" story and reinterpreted it as a drug deal gone wrong in a back alley apartment. Besides a red hoodie for a costume, they also had fake dollar bills and bags of white powder (flour) that they were able to pop and explode all over themselves during the final slow-motion fight scene. It was super easy and very effective. Think about what little details you can add to make your music video stand out.

Backgrounds, including green screens

In the OK Go "Here We Go Again" video, they hung a big silvery tarp on the back wall. (It's tacky enough to make you wonder what was on the wall that they were covering up.) Sometimes the back of the room you're filming in is too cluttered or has things you don't want in the video, so cover it. Or you might be in a photo studio with a variety of different backdrops to choose from.

You might choose to use a green screen that can later be removed digitally (making it transparent) using a "chroma key" effect. With the green screen gone, you can replace it with any other picture or video. A chapter in section three goes into detail about using a green screen.

CREW

We've left the discussion of crew until now, because planning what you need for your shoot is key in determining who you'll need to make it all happen.

The crew is everyone you need to run the equipment and take care of other details (hair, makeup, lights, etc.). On a professional shoot, the crew can range from just a few to dozens of people, each with specialized jobs to support the production process. On a DIY project, the crew may be just you, or just the cast, or it may include people who won't appear in the video.

Even if your plans are simple and you think you can do it all yourself—put the camera on a tripod, pick up guitar, and make the video—it usually goes better with other people along. The right people can help make the process go more smoothly.

I'VE LEARNED THAT MAKING A MUSIC VIDEO TAKES A TEAM! DIY DOESN'T HAVE TO MEAN DO IT ALL YOURSELF, AND THE QUALITY OF THE WORK IS SO MUCH HIGHER WHEN I HAVE A PARTNER OR A FEW SUPPORT PEOPLE. THIS IS ESPECIALLY TRUE WHEN I NEED TO BE IN FRONT OF THE CAMERA, AS GIVING AN ENGAGING PERFORMANCE TAKES MENTAL SPACE AND ENERGY THAT I DON'T WANT TO BE DIVIDING WITH THE MORE TECHNICAL ASPECTS OF SHOOTING A VIDEO.

—Shaudi Bianca Vahdat, American/Iranian Musician and Theatre Artist

Here are a few typical roles on a film crew. Even if you don't anticipate assigning a person to each of these, it's helpful to understand what the major ones are, to make sure someone is covering all the bases.

Producer

The producer ensures everything gets done and makes all the major (non-artistic) decisions.

Director

The director is primarily responsible for all the artistic decisions: what will be done, what it will look like.

Camera operator

Ideally, the camera operator is different from the director: the director is paying attention to what needs to be filmed, and the camera operator is figuring out how to do it. Of course, in many DIY productions, the camera operator, director, and producer are the same person. If you can afford it, a professional camera operator can be a good investment.

Gaffer, or chief lighting technician

If you ever watch film credits, you'll usually see a listing for a gaffer, the person in charge of the lighting. Since it is such a key role, they usually get listed by name, along with their main assistants (for example, the "best boy").

If you're just setting up a couple of lights, you don't need someone specifically in charge of them. However, someone has to set them up, plug them in, turn them on, position them properly, maybe change batteries partway through, and do everything in reverse at the end. With all the different aspects of the shoot you have to coordinate, it can be a real help to have a friend come along and coordinate the lighting. Plus, they get to be called a gaffer. Who wouldn't want that?

Other roles

The list of roles could go on and on, but for a simple shoot, you simply want to make sure someone is in charge of all the little pieces for each of the planning cycles: getting the gear to the location and setting it up, making sure everyone gets where they need to be, checking whatever needs to be checked. It might all be you, or just you and the band, but more hands make for lighter work.

In addition to the people on location during filming (the production crew), you may have helpers working on editing and other post-production tasks, particularly special effects and promotion on social media and other outlets.

SECURITY

We mentioned security above, but it deserves to be its own topic. Cameras and other gear are valuable and easily stolen if you aren't paying attention. Whether it's owned, borrowed, or rented, you always want to know where your gear is. Personal safety might also be a concern, depending on the location; especially for small-time productions, though, it's best to avoid places that don't feel safe.

Place a crew member in charge of keeping things secure, although everyone on the set should stay alert. I had a student who was filming in a park during the day, with his laptop on the ground close by; in a moment of distraction, it was gone.

SCHEDULE AND LOGISTICS

The shooting schedule and logistics is an integral part of all the other planning cycles, since everything and everyone needs to be scheduled and transported to the right place at the right time. Included in your schedule considerations should be daylight hours and weather if you will be dependent on either, in terms of filming or transportation.

I was once involved in a video shoot featuring a flamenco dancer on the beach. Since flamenco stomps can't be heard on sand, the dancer needed a board to dance on. The morning of the shoot it became clear that the board wouldn't fit in anyone's car, so some last-minute trimming was required. That, combined with a few other unexpected delays, meant that instead of being filmed in the early morning hours, cast members had to try not to get heat stroke while performing in July's midday sun.

You may be doing it all yourself, or you may have the luxury of having different people in charge of different aspects. Assuming you can share some of the burden with people you trust to work together and take care of the details, a team of people can ease the burden of scheduling and logistics.

> LOCATION AND LOGISTICS ARE THE HARDEST THINGS ABOUT MAKING A MUSIC VIDEO. ONCE THE CAMERA IS ROLLING, YOU'RE TYPICALLY FINE, BUT THE LEGWORK BEFOREHAND IS WITHOUT QUESTION THE HARDEST—BRAINSTORMING WHAT, WHERE, AND WHEN.
>
> *—Oliver Kersey, British Singer-Songwriter*

While it's tempting to be optimistic, planning for a lot more time than you think it will take (even twice as much), especially if you're doing something new, is often a good strategy. No one complains about finishing work early.

PLANNING AT A GLANCE

The planning cycles

Treatments

- Scripts and beat sheets
- Storyboards
- Shot lists

Locations

- Location scouting
- Scheduling and permissions
- Confirming location details

Budget

Cast

Equipment

- Cameras
- Batteries
- Storage media
- Tripods and other supports
- Lighting gear
- Movement gear
- Audio gear
- Computer and software
- The equipment planning cycles

Art and effects

- Costumes
- Hair and makeup
- Props
- Backgrounds

Crew

- Producer
- Director
- Camera operator
- Gaffer (lighting)
- Others

Security

Schedule and logistics

1.4: CHOOSING A CAMERA

When it comes to tools for making music videos, you can't get more basic than the camera. While it's possible to create a music video without one, using either software or someone else's footage, usually the camera will be your most important piece of equipment.

TYPES OF CAMERAS

The basic types of cameras to consider for filming your music video include the following (approximately from most expensive to least):

- Professional video cameras
- DSLRs or comparable mirrorless cameras (we'll talk about them in more detail after the budget section)
- Drones (aerial quadcopters with video cameras attached)
- Action cameras (small, ruggedized, often waterproof)
- Camcorders (basic video cameras)
- Cell phone cameras (cheapest if you already have a phone)

There are also some specialty cameras, such as 360/VR (virtual reality) cameras for 360-degree videos or ultra-high-speed cameras for extreme slow-motion.

WHICH CAMERA?

When planning the camera to get for a DIY music video shoot, you might find yourself in one of these situations:

1. You have no budget and just want to make a good video, so you'll get the best camera you can borrow (for free) from whatever connections you have.
2. You have some budget, so you want to know what is the best you can get for the money you have.
3. You have exact requirements, so you'll figure out what cameras you need and figure out a way to pay for them.

For the first case (no budget), you need to work your connections and get creative.

- Who in your group most recently upgraded their cell phone? The video cameras in high-end phones keep getting closer to rivaling much larger cameras.
- Who has a parent or other relative who likes to buy the latest gear? They might be hesitant to lend it out, but it's possible they would be happy to have a chance to use it for an interesting project; you could get a camera operator along with the gear.
- Beyond your immediate friends, what about more casual acquaintances? You could put out a notice on social media about what you're planning to do and see if anyone comes forward. Just as with relatives, many times "prosumers" don't have enough good projects to use their fancy equipment on, and they might welcome a chance to use it. (I've seen it happen.)

If you've got a budget or are determined to get one, you have lots of options, so we'll look at different budgets to see what is available for each level: $ (low), $$ (medium), $$$ (high), and $$$$ (probably out of DIY territory, but nice to dream about).

Low budget ($)

If you have just a little to spend toward a camera, here are some options:

- Upgrade your cell phone. If you can get the latest high-end phone as part of a calling plan you are interested in anyway (without having to pay full retail price), that could be a good option. The latest cell phones have high-resolution cameras with sophisticated software enhancements to make remarkably good images from such tiny sensors.

- Rent a large-sensor interchangeable-lens camera (DSLR/mirrorless camera). They are often the camera of choice for filming music videos, and renting them for a few days or a week can be very affordable. Search for "rent DSLR" or "rent video camera" to see what is available in your area or through mail order.

Medium budget ($$)

If you have a little more money to spend, you have a few more options:

- Buy an entry-level DSLR or a comparable mirrorless camera. These will take decent video as well as still photos, and can be used with different lenses (for more $).

- Buy a basic camcorder. These don't have the ability to also take good still photos, and they may not have fully manual options to let you control the picture more precisely, but they can be easy to operate and often have impressive zoom lenses.

- Buy an action camera (such as a GoPro™). They can't be selectively focused (everything is always in focus), and they aren't great in low light, but they can take amazing images when the lighting is good, and their ruggedness and tiny size can lead to some cool shots.

- Buy a basic video-capable drone for aerial shots.

- Rent a higher-end video camera (or DSLR, etc.), along with a variety of lenses.

- Rent two or more video cameras as your budget allows.

High budget ($$$)

If you have some money saved up or have a generous benefactor, here are some of the best choices for making a music video:

- Buy a high-end DSLR or mirrorless camera, along with lenses and accessories.

- Buy a really good drone.

- Rent a professional video camera kit (including lenses, tripods, etc.). Keep in mind that a pro camera will be the least user-friendly, so you'll need to spend the effort to learn how to use it, or also hire someone who can operate the camera effectively.

Wishful-thinking budget ($$$$)

- Buy a pro video camera.

- Rent an even better video camera, along with an operator. (For any budget, there's always a camera too expensive to buy that you might be able to rent.)

- Get multiple cameras, for other angles, backup, and b-roll (extra shots that aren't the main shot), or as many cameras of each type (DSLR, action, drone, 360/VR, etc.) as you need.

DSLRS VS. MIRRORLESS CAMERAS

The preferred class of cameras for many budget-minded indie filmmakers, including music video directors, is a little difficult to describe, because it consists of two types of cameras. These are cameras with relatively large sensors (larger sensors usually mean better images) and the ability to use different lenses. They also can take both high-quality still photos as well as excellent video, with fully manual controls and lots of options for different filmmaking needs.

We'll start with a bit of history. Before there were digital cameras, the most popular professional still-image cameras were SLRs, or single-lens reflex cameras. These cameras were made to allow the photographer to look through the actual lens that would produce the final image (the "SL" part) rather than through a separate view-finder window that would give a slightly different image than what was actually recorded on film. The "reflex" part referred to the mirror in the camera that made this possible.

When digital electronic sensors replaced film, the SLR configuration still produced the most accurate preview of the image to be recorded, so high-end SLRs became DSLRs. The presence of the digital sensor meant video as well as still photos were possible, so that capability was eventually added to DSLRs. The size of the sensor was equal to the size of the 35mm film it replaced (called "full frame"), or sometimes a little smaller ("APS-C"), large enough to create professional-quality images.

Smaller-sensor digital cameras that were too small and/or inexpensive for SLR mechanics used viewfinders with digital screens that attempted to recreate what the sensor was recording. Even so, the screens were not nearly as good as the actual view you would get with a DSLR.

Eventually, digital screen technology improved to the point where a mirrorless camera could be created that was smaller than a DSLR (since the mirror mechanism requires a fair amount of space), but with comparable quality and features. These are sometimes called "mirrorless" cameras, although any digital camera that is not a DSLR, including phones, drones, point-and-shoots, and action cams, are all mirrorless cameras, so the term is a little confusing.

These mirrorless cameras can be full frame, APS-C, or with a smaller (but still relatively large) sensor known as MFT or micro four-thirds. They use interchangeable lenses that give them the flexibility and advantages of DSLRs; in some cases, mirrorless cameras are surpassing the capabilities of DSLRs, particularly for taking video.

If you shop for a professional-quality digital camera that can take stills or video and uses interchangeable lenses, it may be a DSLR or mirrorless, although mirrorless cameras are seeing more developments and may eventually eliminate the need for the SLR mechanism. Any given camera will have different capabilities and advantages, but a mirrorless camera should be a little smaller than a DSLR.

LENSES

If you have an interchangeable-lens camera and you have the option to use different lenses (buying, borrowing, or renting), you'll have more flexibility to customize the shots you can capture. We'll review some of the basics about lenses before looking at recommendations for specific situations.

Prime vs. Zoom

Lenses are of two basic types: Prime and Zoom. A prime lens has only one focal length, such as 50mm, meaning it has only one field of view, and only one "magnification" level. Prime lenses tend to be smaller, lighter, and cheaper than similar zoom lenses, with a larger maximum aperture and often a better image quality. A zoom lens has a changeable focal length (such as from 35mm to 70mm), so you get more than one field of view with one lens.

Normal vs. Wide vs. Telephoto

You can also classify lenses based on the focal length: 50mm is a "normal" length for a full-frame camera, with a field of view (how wide the camera sees) similar to what the human eye can see. 35mm and below is "wide," meaning it sees a wider field of view than your eyes would normally see, and over 100mm is usually called "tele-photo," giving you a narrower field of view, resulting in an appearance of more magnification.

To further complicate things, the "normalness" of the field of view depends on the size of the camera sensor (or, in the old days, the size of the film). A smaller sensor has a smaller "normal" focal length, so, for example, a 25mm lens on a micro-four-thirds camera is equivalent to 50mm on a full-frame camera. Normal for an APS-C camera is between these two.

Lens Cost and Quality

Lenses can vary widely in cost; in some cases, they can cost more than your camera itself. Lens costs go up based on their construction quality, particularly the quality of the optics, as well as their maximum aperture or f-stop. The extra cost produces sharper, clearer images with a wider variety of options. In particular, a wider maximum aperture provides the ability to shoot in lower light or with a shallower depth of field.

In general, you get what you pay for, so you can get cheap or expensive lenses from a given manufacturer, although there are some third-party lenses that are very good for less money. Here are some general rules about lenses:

- Images from cheaper lenses are not as sharp as those from more expensive lenses.

- Zoom lenses (with a range of focal lengths, expressed in mm) produce images that are not as sharp as those from prime lenses (with only one focal length).

- "Kit" lenses (the ones that come bundled with a camera) tend to be the cheapest lenses—often still pretty good, but with lots of room for improvement.

- Every lens can have different sharpness levels at different f-stops, and potentially at different focal distances (the distance from the camera to the thing you are focusing on).

- Zoom lenses have different sharpness levels at different focal lengths (zoom settings), and often the extremes are the worst—that is, a 35-70mm zoom may be sharper at 50 or 60mm than at 35 or 70mm.

- Sharpness can also vary among lenses that are the same model because of manufacturing irregularities, prior damage/abuse, etc.

- Many modern lenses come with internal lens stabilization, which can help reduce shake in moving shots. There is usually an option to turn the stabilization on or off.

Which lens should you use?

If there is a choice of lenses to use, consider these factors:

- How shallow do you want the depth of field? That is, do you want just the subject to be sharply in focus and the background blurry? If that is the case, you'll want a lens with a wide maximum aperture, which means a lower f-stop number (1.8 or 2.8 rather than 3.5 or 4.2, for example).

- How close do you want to get to your subject? If you want extreme close-ups, you'll want a lens with a small minimum focus distance, which usually means a smaller focal length (35mm or less). If you want or need to be far away, a longer focal length (100mm or more) will be better.

- How wide do you want your field of view to be? A wide field of view comes from a smaller focal length, and narrow field of view from a longer focal length.

- How much light will you have for filming? If you are hoping for some low-light shots, a wider aperture (f-stop of 2.8 or less) will give you more flexibility.

- If you will have moving shots, camera shake will be more extreme with longer focal lengths. In any case, using lenses with stabilization will help.

TEST AND PRACTICE WITH YOUR GEAR

Whichever camera and other equipment you decide to use, be sure to test it out and practice with it before you need it for an actual shoot. If you have more than one lens available, try out each one in different lighting and other situations to understand what sorts of images they produce. Get familiar with all the key functions of whatever cameras you buy, borrow, or rent.

The worst case scenario is not knowing which button to push or dial to turn when a live performance is about to start and you can't delay it while you figure out how to use your equipment. Even if you control the schedule, it's not fun for anyone if you have people standing around while you try to remember how to fix the white balance.

CHOOSING A CAMERA AT A GLANCE

Types of cameras
- Pro video cameras
- DSLRs, mirrorless cameras
- Drones
- Action cams
- Camcorders
- Cell phone cameras

Which camera?
- No budget: cell phone, borrow (relatives, friends)
- Low budget: cell phone upgrade, rent
- Medium budget: buy, rent better
- High budget: buy better, rent upscale
- Mega budget: buy upscale, rent even better, get multiple cameras

DSLRs vs. mirrorless cameras

Lenses
- Prime vs. zoom
- Normal vs. wide vs. telephoto
- Lens cost and quality
- Which lens should you use?

Test and practice with your gear

2.0: PRODUCTION

Filming your video

SHOOTING IS THE MOST ENJOYABLE PART ABOUT MAKING A MUSIC VIDEO.
YOU USUALLY GO OUT THERE WITH IDEAS OF SHOTS YOU WANT.
WHEN FILMING DAY COMES, YOU OFTEN WALK AWAY WITH SHOTS YOU
WEREN'T EXPECTING TO GET. THOSE ARE OFTEN THE BEST ONES.

– Josh Wallace, Singer-Songwriter, Percussionist

The production phase is where video making really gets interesting. It can be where the fun ramps up, and where you see that your planning really paid off. Or it might be where you realize that your preparation was inadequate, or that you imagined the situation to be completely different than it turned out to be.

A student of mine, Steve Umculo, decided he wanted to do a stop-motion lyric video for a class assignment. He planned it out well, and it seemed to him like a great idea: Go to the beach and spell out the lyrics using things found on the sand: shells, rocks, seaweed balls, and the like. When we talked about his plan, I suggested it might turn out to be a lot more work than he expected, so we discussed some ways to reduce what I thought would be an interminable production phase.

He considered my suggestions and modified his plan, but still had the same basic idea when he started filming. It soon became apparent that he had seriously underestimated how long it would take. In Steve's own words:

I THOUGHT TO MYSELF, "HOW HARD COULD IT BE? YOU JUST HAVE TO SET UP A
CAMERA, GET SOME STUFF AND THEN MOVE THE STUFF AROUND? RIGHT?" SO I
SET OFF INTO THE BIG BAD WORLD TO UNDERTAKE THIS SEEMINGLY MINOR TASK.

I TOOK MY FRIEND CLIFF AND ABOUT $1000 WORTH OF CAMERA EQUIPMENT
ALONG WITH ME TO THE BEACH (AS YOU DO) TO START THIS PROCESS. I
THOUGHT, "COOL, AN HOUR AT THE BEACH AND THEN I CAN MOVE ON TO THE
PARK, THEN OUTSIDE THE SCHOOL AND I CAN SMASH THIS VIDEO IN ONE DAY."
OH, HOW NAÏVE YOU ARE, PAST STEVE! IT TOOK ME ABOUT AN HOUR TO FIND THE
PERFECT LOCATION AND SET UP THE EQUIPMENT. THEN THE FUN STARTED....

ONCE THIS SUPPOSED "ONE-HOUR" (ACTUALLY SEVEN-HOUR)
PROCESS ENDED, MY ENTIRE BODY WAS RED [FROM SUNBURN]
AND I HAD FINISHED ONLY HALF-A-VERSE. I THOUGHT, "NO WAY.
I'M THROWING IN THE TOWEL." BUT I GOT BACK TO SCHOOL AND PUT
TOGETHER THAT HALF-A-VERSE OF MY METICULOUS CREATION AND
IT LOOKED TOO GOOD NOT TO USE....

In the end, he stuck with it (and I gave him a deadline extension on the assignment), but he did have to compromise even his modified vision, despite putting in at least 70 hours—ten times his original estimate—on the project. (Check out the finished music video, "Answer" [the stop-motion lyric version] by Steve Umculo to see how it turned out.)

In this section of the book, we'll explore the areas the director and camera operator will want to focus on to make the production as professional as possible. We'll go over "Loud Dogs," a poem to help you remember the things to keep in mind while shooting, then talk about the individual pieces: lighting, scene composition, camera movement, depth of field, and camera settings and specifications.

The final chapter in this section, "Movie time," is where you pick up the camera and make it all happen.

2.1: LOUD DOGS ON THE SET

A way to remember the little details during filming

We've had our hands full with lots of checklists for managing all the do-ahead stages: We've looked at the plan, reconsidered the GAT vision (Goals, Art, Tech), and double-checked the equipment. The next step is keeping track of everything that happens during filming, including setting up the camera so it will do the best job possible and get the shots you want.

> WE DO NOT NECESSARILY NEED HUGE TEAMS TO PRODUCE VIDEOS, WHICH MEANS LESS ORGANIZATION, BUT IT ALSO MEANS YOU NEED TO BE AN EXPERT IN MANY MORE FIELDS. YOU NEED TO KNOW ABOUT CAMERAS, LIGHTING, COLOR THEORY, EDITING, GRADING, COMPOSITING, ETC. WHEN YOU ARE ON A LOW BUDGET AND DOING THIS ALONE.
>
> *–Pierce Warnecke, Sound and Video Artist and Educator*

This is where you get down to the nuts and bolts. How can you make sure it all goes smoothly? What separates a professional-looking shot from an amateurish one?

You need *Loud Dogs*!

LOUD DOGS

Loud Dogs Are
By My Door!

Could Loud Bulls
Torment Me More?

Maybe Someone
Will Fix It For

Me!

Loud Dogs is a mnemonic poem—a memory aid to learn (or have on your phone somewhere) so you can remember key aspects of the production process.

Each word in the poem will help you remember an important step in the preparation for filming:

Loud	Lighting
Dogs	Distance
Are	Angle
By	Balance
My	Movement
Door	Depth of field
Could	Card (memory)
Loud	Lens
Bulls	Battery
Torment	Tripod plate
Me	Manual control
More	Manual focus
Maybe	Movie size
Someone	Shutter speed
Will	White balance
Fix	F-stop
It	ISO
For	Focus
Me!	Movie time!

With *Loud Dogs* in mind, you'll remember the elements that will make your shots better and your day of filming more successful. The poem covers these four essential aspects of your filming:

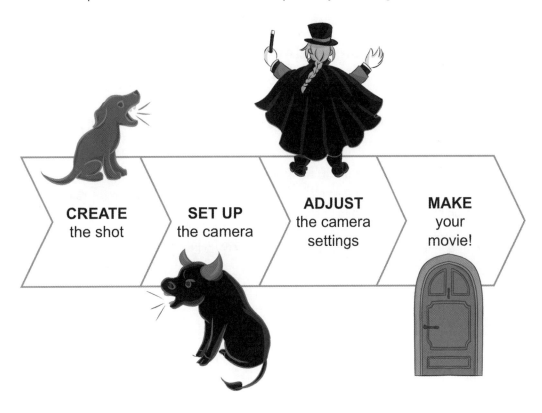

Create the shot *(Loud Dogs Are By My Door)*: How you set up your scene is one of the keys to looking more professional and less amateurish. That is, from the beginning of your video to the very end, you have a rectangle (the screen of the video) that you are creating to show the world. How do you make that rectangle look as good as possible?

The topics represented by this first line of *Loud Dogs* will be the focus of the majority of the chapters in this section: **Lighting**, **Distance**, **Angle**, **Balance**, **Movement**, and **Depth of field**.

Set up the Camera *(Could Loud Bulls Torment Me More?)*: This includes the physical components: **Card**, **Lens**, **Battery**, **Tripod plate**, **Manual control**, **Manual focus**. Camera setup will differ by camera model and type, but there are general guidelines that can be helpful. We'll talk more about them in a later chapter.

Adjust the camera settings *(Maybe Someone Will Fix It For)*: Once the camera is all put together, you'll make adjustments to **Movie size**, **Shutter speed**, **White balance**, **F-stop**, **ISO**, and **Focus**.

The technical details will be the focus of one of the last chapters in this section. While you can get by without knowing them all, this section can provide you with understanding that will help you get the best shots possible.

Make your movie! *(Me!)*: In the **Movie time** chapter, we'll go over some practical advice for everyone involved (directors and performers) when the camera starts rolling.

2.2: LIGHTING FUNDAMENTALS

LOUD Dogs Are By My Door

Lighting

Light is the foundation of any kind of visual media, and one of the most important considerations in creating an effective music video. Light is so basic we don't tend to notice it, but in the best photographs, paintings, and movies, lighting usually plays a key role. Take a winning music video and remove the purposefully added lighting, or even do the lighting badly, and it will lose most or all of its appeal.

Lighting is critical not only to help the viewer see what you want them to see, but also to create the mood for your video. Lighting can also give depth to your scene and create a more cinematic look.

On a professional movie set or music video shoot, an entire team is devoted to getting the lighting right. If you are a one-person DIY production, that may seem intimidating, but you'll find here the information you need to make your project look its best.

Because lighting is such an important subject, we have devoted two chapters to it. This chapter gets into the fundamentals of lighting, taking a more theoretical and technical approach. If you want your lighting to make your video stand out, you'll want to dive into this chapter.

The next chapter is a guide to actually lighting your music video, going through the four key steps to creating good lighting:

1. Goals (What do you want your lighting to do?)
2. Assessment (What lighting do you have?)
3. Plan (What do you need to do with your lighting to meet your goals?)
4. Action (Do it!)

Each one of these steps will be easier and more effective if you understand the fundamentals of lighting: the attributes of light and the artistic functions of lighting.

ATTRIBUTES OF LIGHT

For the purposes of lighting a music video, we can describe light by looking at six basic attributes:

1. Color
2. Direction
3. Brightness
4. Hardness
5. Spread
6. Pattern

Understanding and controlling these attributes will help you create the look and mood that you want in your music video.

Color

When we talk about the color of light, we can dig a little deeper and look at three important aspects of light:

- Color temperature
- Color quality
- Hue

Color temperature

Color temperature refers to how "warm" or "cold" a light is, particularly what we think of as "white" light. White light can tend toward being yellowish (warm), such as the light from a flame or a tungsten light bulb, or bluish (cold), or somewhere in between.

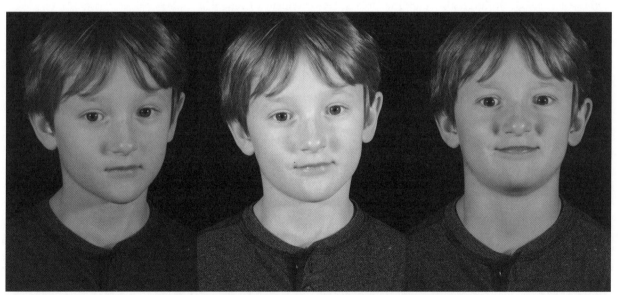

Warm, sunlight balanced, and cool color temperatures

If you buy LED lights (or certain fluorescent lights), you may notice that many of them list a color temperature, given as some thousands of degrees Kelvin (or °K). 3200°K is a warm light, while 5500 to 6500°K is a bluer or more "natural" light, closer to daylight from the sun. A tungsten or incandescent bulb is probably 2500-3500°K.

Why should you care about color temperature for your music video? First, a video camera will do something called "white balance," the camera's attempt to figure out what color "white" really is. (We talk more about white balance in the Camera Settings chapter.) If the camera doesn't get the white balance right, everything and everyone in your shot will look wrong, either too yellow or too blue.

Second, when you set up lights (see the next chapter), you will want to understand color temperature so you don't mix color temperatures without intending to. If you want the skin tones of your musicians to look right, all the lights shining on them should be a similar color temperature so the camera can set the white balance correctly. If you have sunlight from a window in one direction, and incandescent bulbs lighting the band from another direction, something's going to look funky. Even if it looks fine to our eyes, the camera's sensor is less forgiving, so the recorded video will have colors that are "off."

ONE MAJOR CHALLENGE WHEN MAKING A MUSIC VIDEO IS KEEPING CONSISTENCY IN THE COLORS WHEN TRANSITIONING FROM SCENE TO SCENE AND/OR WHEN CHANGING ANGLES WHILE KEEPING THE QUALITY HIGH (CLARITY IN THE PICTURE), EVEN WHEN THE CIRCUMSTANCES ARE NOT PERFECT (PROPER LIGHTS, ETC.).

–Christos Stylianides, Cypriot Music Producer, Mixing Engineer

Ideally, it's valuable to have a light meter to tell you the temperature of all of your lights, but for a DIY approach, just knowing what is coming through the window vs. what to expect from a type of bulb is enough to avoid most problems.

If you plan on shooting during the day but want to add supplemental light, getting lights or bulbs that have a Kelvin listing in the 5000-6000°K range is a good idea. If you're using tungsten lights (regular incandescent or halogen), make sure all your lights are a similar temperature (around 3000°K), whether "warm" LEDs or fluorescents.

Deliberately mixing different color temperatures can be an effective way to add depth to your scene, with bluer lights in the rear and warmer ones up front. We'll talk more about that in the next chapter.

Color quality

Just getting the color temperature right isn't enough to make sure that whites look properly white (and skin tones don't look greenish or purplish). Color quality is another element to consider.

"Natural" light, either from the sun or from incandescent bulbs, renders the colors we accept as standard, or what we consider to be correct. With fluorescent or LED lights, some parts of the spectrum they emit may render colors in a way that looks incorrect. (Our eyes make adjustments and don't tend to notice, but the camera will notice.)

A fairly common way to measure color quality is CRI (color rendering index). A CRI of 100 is a perfect score, which is what the sun would get. Lights made especially for video or other applications where accurate color is important often have CRIs of 90 or 95. A compact fluorescent from the hardware store, unless it specifically lists a high CRI, may have a CRI of 50 to 70, and a standard LED bulb may have a CRI in the 80s.

A high CRI doesn't mean the light will render color perfectly, and there is some debate about the right measure to use, but it's good enough for our purposes. If you're using something other than light from the sun or tungsten bulbs to light your video, look for bulbs with a CRI of 90 or above, and you'll get colors that look the most natural.

Hue

Hue describes colors in the more traditional meaning of the word—red, orange, yellow, green, blue, and so on. With lights of different hues in your video, color temperature and CRI aren't really issues, because you aren't going for natural colors anyway.

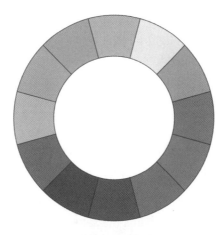

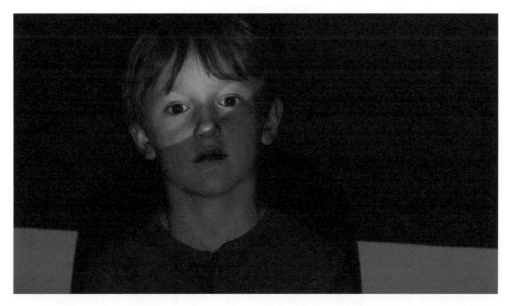

Adding lights of different hues, either to complement your "white" lights or in place of them, can be a good way to add variety and depth to your scene. For example, if you want to create a nightclub scene for your video, then maybe using only colored (non-white) lights will get you the look you want.

Adding gels, colored pieces of special plastic, to the front of the lights is the most common way to change their hue. (More about gels in the next chapter.) Color can also be changed using a movie projector, by creating a video of one or more colors and using the projector as a colored light source for your scene. Another option is to buy pre-colored lights, particularly RGB (Red Green Blue) LED lights that let you modify the light hue to just about any color imaginable.

Direction

The direction of the light toward your subject can make a big difference in the mood or feel of the shot. Many situations, especially indoors, will have light from multiple directions because of windows, overhead lights, light reflected off white walls, and so on. This will make the scene look "normal," with everything easily visible but without much drama.

If you want a more intense or cinematic mood to the shot, block out the ambient light and restrict the light direction for different effects. For example, set up light to come from a single direction: directly overhead, directly in front, from the bottom, from one side, or even from behind to create a silhouette. Each of these will create noticeably different moods.

We'll cover the specifics of using lighting direction in the Lighting Placement section of the next chapter.

Brightness

Brightness refers to how strong or bright a light is. (You could also say "intensity," although they are slightly different concepts.) Very bright lights will produce the whitest whites (assuming color temperature and CRI are taken care of) and the richest colors, while lowering brightness will make everything look progressively duller, grayer, and darker until you get to black.

Brightness, combined with direction, has a big effect on the mood of your video. Overall brightness is also technically important to make sure you have enough light for your camera to record the scene the way you want it. It's possible to have too much light, but unless you're filming outside in the sun, the more common problem is usually too little light.

If two or more lights of equal brightness are pointed at the same object from different directions, shadows will be reduced, making the object look flatter. If the lights have different levels of brightness, such as in the three-point lighting setup discussed in the next chapter, the object will look more three-dimensional because of the shadows on the side with the weaker light.

Some video lights have variable brightness, so you can change the brightness using a dial, a button, or software. Assuming your lights are at their brightest, you can increase brightness by moving the lights closer to the subject, or by increasing the number of lights. Of course, you can decrease brightness by doing the opposite, moving them farther away or turning off some lights.

Because lights are the most common pieces of gear to fail during a shoot, and because you may find that the scene you're shooting is darker than expected, it's a good idea to bring along more lights than you think you'll need.

Hardness

The hardness of a light is another factor in creating the mood of your scene. Hardness refers to the edge that separates light from shadow. A hard light produces a clear, distinct line where the light stops and the shadow begins. A softer light has a fuzzier border between the light and dark, and the softest light creates the most gradual transition from light to shadow.

The main thing that determines hardness is the size of the light source in relation to your subject: Bigger lights give softer light than smaller lights. If you move a bigger light farther from your subject, then it becomes relatively smaller, so the light becomes harder.

The best example of this is sunlight. On a cloudless day at noon, the sun produces a hard light, because the light comes directly from an (apparently) tiny object that is so far away. On an overcast day, the most immediate light source is the huge cloud-filled sky, since the light from the distant sun is diffused and scattered by the much nearer clouds. This produces a very soft light with shadows that are indistinct.

For a music video, a hard light will create a mood that is more dramatic and stark, while a soft light will have a mellowing effect. In many cases, you'll want something that is somewhere in between—not too hard, but not too soft either. That may mean adding a light modifier or diffuser to your lights.

A diffuser is usually a large white translucent panel between your light source and your subject that scatters the light, much the same way that clouds do to sunlight. You can use professional "soft boxes," although a little DIY ingenuity can get you a long way, using white fabric or even a white shower curtain. (See the next chapter for suggestions.)

Spread

The spread of light refers to the width of the beam of light from your light source. Sometimes you'll want the widest spread possible—180 degrees if shining from the side of a scene—but other times, a narrower beam will let you light different parts of the scene differently.

The narrowest beams might come from laser lights, useful for decorations or accents. On a larger scale, spotlights use special lenses to focus and restrict the light to an adjustable narrow beam.

If you are lighting your scene with household light bulbs, a regular bulb shape will produce a full-spread 360-degree light, although that will be restricted if you use a reflector. A flood-type lamp will give a narrower V-shaped beam, probably between 70 and 90 degrees. A flat LED panel should produce close to a full 180-degree spread, although they sometimes come with "barn door" reflectors that can narrow the beam. You can imitate a spotlight effect by using a video of a white dot on a black background projected onto your subject. (See the Lighting video for an example.)

Spread is important for creating mood and depth in your scene. For example, if you have three musicians on stage, shining three narrow lights that illuminate only their faces will produce a much different mood than shining broad lights that show everything on stage equally. Lights with restricted spread, when shone on a back wall, can make interesting patterns that give depth to a scene. Even a lampshade on a table lamp produces a much different light than a bare bulb, partly because of how the spread is controlled.

Pattern

Most of the time, light will have no pattern—that is, within its beam, it will just be a solid brightness, or maybe brighter in the center and fading a bit toward the edges.

A pattern appears when the solid beam of light is interrupted with alternating areas of light and dark. For example, a common light pattern is alternating horizontal strips of light and dark produced by a window shade. You could also have a grid pattern, a series of smaller circles of light, or a random pattern of light shining through the leaves of a tree.

In the world of theater, these patterns are created on stage using things called gobos, flags, or cookies—patterned plates or sheets of metal that are placed in front of lights. In the DIY world, you could get a pattern by shining a light through a part of a fence, a tree branch, or even a piece of cardboard with holes cut in it. These will often create fuzzy, indistinct patterns, but more focused patterns can be created using a projector showing a static or animated video of any white/black patterns you create.

LIGHTING FUNDAMENTALS AT A GLANCE

Attributes of light

- Color
  - Color temperature
  - Color quality
  - Hue
- Direction
- Brightness
- Hardness
- Spread
- Pattern

2.3: LIGHTING GUIDE

LOUD Dogs Are By My Door (part 2)

Now that you understand more about the different attributes of light and how they affect the scene, we'll consider specific steps for lighting your music video professionally using whatever you have available.

There are four main steps when approaching a video lighting project:

1. Goals (What do you want your lighting to do?)
2. Assessment (What lighting do you have?)
3. Plan (What do you need to do with your lighting to meet your goals?)
4. Action (Do it!)

1. GOALS (WHAT DO YOU WANT?)

At its most basic, lighting has three primary goals:

- View: Can you clearly see all the objects you want to see?
- Mood: Does the lighting create the right mood and tell the story you want to tell?
- Depth: Can you make the scene more interesting with layers that are lit differently?

View

Consciously controlling the light as much as possible is the best way to make sure the audience sees what you want them to see while getting the best possible image.

In everyday life, seeing is not generally a problem. We have either natural or artificial light wherever we go. We don't pay attention to it unless we are in a situation where we can't see what we want to see—perhaps a narrow alley late at night, or a dark storeroom with a hard-to-find light switch.

These issues are relevant to creating a music video as well, but at a more extreme level, because most camera sensors are not nearly as good as our eyes at seeing in the dark.

Even inexpensive cell phones or tiny action cams will do a good job of recording a scene if the area is fully lit by daylight. But in low-light situations our eyes have no problem with, including indoors or in the shade, a digital camera sensor typically won't have enough dynamic range, which means details in the shadows or in the bright spots (or both) will be lost and replaced with pure black and pure white. Cameras will also record more digital "noise" (random variations and mistakes) in poor light.

Mood

The light you start with at your location may not be the light required to create a certain mood. Controlling and modifying that lighting can help you create drama, serenity, or excitement.

Consider the different attributes of light (discussed in the previous chapter) and the ways they can help set specific moods:

- Color: Warm-colored lights can bring a warm feeling to a scene, while cool lights can do the opposite. A dark blue light can create the subdued mood of being outdoors at night in the moonlight. Red can be used for danger or excitement. Flashing colored lights can help create a vibrant club atmosphere.

- Direction: A hard, bright light coming from just one side in a dark space (traditionally called "chiaroscuro," or "bright/dark") can create high drama and mystery. Strong backlighting can create mysterious silhouettes.

- Brightness: Excessively bright light can be used to create a heavenly space, or one with a clinical feel. Low lights with many shadows can create a mood of danger.

- Hardness: Hard lights work well in "hard" scenes, creating tension and encouraging violence. Soft lighting is better for more sensitive or sensual scenes.

- Spread: Broad, even lighting helps create a mood of safety and well-being. Tight, limited lighting can have the opposite effect.

- Pattern: Creative use of patterned lighting can indicate rain, lightning, resting under a leafy canopy, or spying through a grate.

Whatever mood you want to create, controlling the lighting—the color, direction, brightness, and more—will be key to making it happen.

Depth

If you want something more than a flat, two-dimensional scene, use different layers of color or texture at different distances from the camera to create a strong three-dimensional environment and more cinematic feel. Soft, even lighting, coming from all sides and eliminating shadows, contributes to a flat look in your scene. Depth can come by varying the different attributes of light at different distances from the camera.

For example, cool or bluer lights tend to recede from our view, so if you have the foreground lit with warmer lights but the background in cooler lights, or if you add lights of different hues (reds, yellows, more intense blues) at different spots in the scene, particularly on a back wall, it will enhance the feeling of depth.

The other attributes of light can also be effective at enhancing the feeling of depth. For example:

- Direction: Light coming primarily from one side in the foreground and from the other side in the background

- Brightness: A bright foreground, dark middle ground, and dimly lit background

- Hardness: Hard shadows near the camera, but much softer light further away

- Spread: Tight spotlights on specific parts of the scene, some nearer the camera and some farther away

- Pattern: Using a template to shine a pattern of diagonal lines on the back wall, while the foreground is lit evenly from overhead

2. ASSESSMENT (WHAT DO YOU HAVE?)

Once you've carefully considered your goals in terms of view, mood, and depth, you can better evaluate your current situation and determine what needs to change, if anything, to get the look you want at your location. Whenever possible, plan to visit it in advance, preferably at a time similar to when you plan to shoot, so you can clearly understand what light you will have to work with.

If you're planning to shoot indoors or out at a time of day when the outdoor light changes rapidly (dawn and dusk), or if the sky is intermittently cloudy and sunny, consider how that will affect what you want to accomplish. If the sun is bright and clear in the sky, think about the hardness of the shadows and the contrast between being in sun and shade.

If you'll be indoors, look at the light coming through windows as well as overhead or other existing lights. Remember differences in color temperature of windows vs. indoor lights, and the lower color quality of typical fluorescent lights. Notice what direction the light is coming from.

3. PLAN (WHAT DO YOU NEED TO DO?)

After understanding what you're working with and what you want to change, the next step is to plan your lighting setup. Here are some areas to consider:

Types of lights

When deciding between different types of lights, it's helpful to understand the properties of each and how they differ from one another.

Tungsten or incandescent

Tungsten lights were the most common type of household light for many decades. They emit light because a tungsten filament burns inside a vacuum, giving off both a bright, warm light and a lot of heat.

These lights are usually low priced, dimmable, and good at rendering color (high CRI). Their main disadvantage is that they only produce light of a lower color temperature (yellow-orangish), and they get very hot, making them more dangerous, less efficient (less light per unit of energy), and shorter lived. Also, if you want to gel the lights (modify the color by covering with a plastic sheet), you have to use special gels designed for the high temperatures. Tungsten lights are increasingly being replaced by CFLs (compact fluorescent bulbs) and LED bulbs.

Halogen

Halogen lights are a type of tungsten light that includes halogen gas. They have similar advantages and disadvantages to regular tungsten, although they are brighter and tend to last longer. They are also relatively inefficient and much hotter, making them more of a fire and burn hazard.

If you need very bright, relatively inexpensive lights, halogen work lights can be a good solution, as long as you handle them carefully.

Fluorescent

Fluorescent lights (including CFLs, or compact fluorescent lights) produce much less heat than tungsten lights, so they are more efficient and have a much longer expected life. You can get fluorescent bulbs that are dimmable and in a variety of color temperatures, including ones with high CRI. Typical fluorescents in homes and commercial buildings often don't specify the color temperature, making it difficult to match them with other types of lights, and their color rendering can be quite poor.

Because fluorescent lights require a ballast to regulate the electrical current, they can sometimes produce a buzzing sound. They contain mercury and are generally considered to be hazardous waste for disposal. They can also have a flicker that may not be visible to the naked eye, but potentially visible to a video camera. These factors mean that generic fluorescents can create problems for a video shoot, but in general, fluorescents that are made specifically for filming — with a specified color temperature, high CRI, and no flicker — can be a good option.

LED

LEDs, or light-emitting diode lights, have many advantages compared to other commonly available lights and are the emerging preference for regular as well as video lighting. They are the most efficient and longest lasting of common lights and can be made in a variety of hues and color temperatures, including whites with a high CRI. Video-specific LED lights are often variable temperature as well as dimmable to match a variety of settings. They are also more compact and durable than most other light types, and can usually run on batteries. If they are available, LEDs are a great choice.

Lighting placement

When considering where to put your lights, there are some standard terms that will be helpful.

Key light

Most sets have a "key" light, which is the main and brightest light. A key light can be placed anywhere, but a 45-degree angle (shining from the midpoint between straight ahead and directly to the side) will give a nice depth to your subject.

The key light can also be placed directly to the side of the subject (90 degrees) for more drama. If this is the only light, it is called a "low key" that creates a "chiaroscuro" effect, often used in classic art for dramatic scenes.

Fill light

The fill light is weaker than the key light, but helps fill in the shadows caused by the key light, if you don't want the shaded part of your subject to be completely in the dark. If the key light is at an angle on one side of your subject, the fill light is typically at the opposite side.

Fill light can also come from reflective surfaces, including white walls opposite the key light, or light surfaces set up to bounce light to the darker side of your subject.

Rim or hair light

The rim or hair light is near the back, often mounted high, pointed forward toward the back of your subject to help add more separation between the subject and the background. The rim light is normally placed so it can't be seen by the camera.

Three-point lighting

If you combine a key light, fill light, and rim light, you have the classic "three-point lighting" that gives good illumination to a single subject or small group.

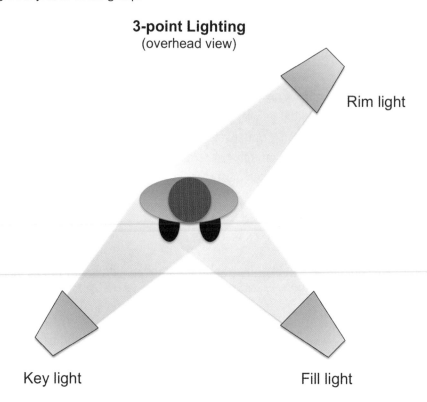

3-point Lighting
(overhead view)

Rim light

Key light   Fill light

Besides this classic setup, there are many other ways to point your lights. They will each have a different effect, so instead of pointing all your lights from the front, take time to experiment. Just remember that if you want a cinematic look, plan to restrict the light direction so it doesn't come from everywhere at once.

Practicals

Any light that appears on the set (visible to the camera) is called a "practical." These are effective for creating mood, although they can help light the subjects as well. Practicals may include hanging lights, desk lamps, candles, string lights (such as Christmas or fairy lights), or even flashlights.

If your practicals are strong lights shining directly at the camera, they may cause flares or silhouettes, making the subject more difficult to see (which may or may not be the effect you want).

Back light

The back light shines on the background, particularly if there is a back wall or backdrop, to help give more depth and interest to a scene. If the area is open, practical lights behind the subject can also be used.

Lighting stands and modifiers

Some lights come with their own stands, but video lights usually need to be attached to something.

Light stands

Regular light stands are lightweight and easy to place almost anywhere, helping you get just the look you want. A useful addition to a light stand is a ball-head mount that lets you tilt and position your light.

Tripods

Tripods are typically used for cameras, but they can also be handy for positioning lights. They don't go as high as a light stand, and you may need an adapter to attach a light to it.

Small flexible-leg tripods can be especially useful for attaching a light to a beam, pole, or other handy object.

Diffusers

A diffuser is some sort of translucent sheet, usually plastic or fabric, to help soften light, since light from a bare bulb is often harder than you want for your scene. An example is a soft box, a lightweight, foldable "box" that attaches to a light stand and fits around a light, with a white fabric front to diffuse the light. You can also make a diffuser by hanging a piece of white fabric or shower curtain on a line or on a rod between two light stands or other poles, and positioning your light behind it to shine through onto your subject.

While diffusers are great for softening light, they also reduce the brightness of your light, so keep that in mind. If using a curtain diffuser, you can place multiple lights behind the curtain to increase the total light output.

Gels

Gels are colored sheets of plastic that can change the color temperature or hue of your light. They are typically heat resistant for using on traditional lights, which are hotter than modern LEDs or fluorescents. If you buy movie gels, they come in standard colors, including ones that can change the color temperature of a light to a specific degree. If you use LED lights, you might be able to get away with using inexpensive colored cellophane or some other plastic, but you should test to make sure.

Depending on the light, it can be a challenge to figure out a way to attach them to the light, so you may have to get creative. If your light has cooling vents, make sure the plastic does not block the vents in any way. Also, as with diffusers, adding gels decreases the brightness of the light, so you may need to add more lights to compensate.

Reflectors

Reflectors bounce light from another source. They can add light from a source that is already adding light to a scene by reflecting on the opposite side of the subject, or they can greatly soften (and reduce the brightness of a light) that is shined directly on them. Reflectors include special umbrellas made for that purpose, but also white walls or sheets of white foam-core board.

4. ACTION (DO IT!)

Here are a few tips to keep in mind as you put your lighting plan into practice:

Leave enough time (probably more than you think you need) to get everything set up, including time to change everything around when the end result doesn't match your original goals.

Remember power! If you have battery-powered lights, be sure the batteries are fully charged, and bring extras if possible. If you are using AC power, make certain you know where to plug in, and that you have plenty of (properly rated, not too thin) extension cords with lots of outlets to plug in what you need.

With modern (LED and CFL) lights on smallish sets, the power requirements for lighting usually aren't more than a basic system can handle. High demand from power-sucking traditional lights, or many lights on a really large set, can increase the risk of tripping circuits or shorting something out.

As I've mentioned before, in my experience, if something is going to fail prematurely during your shoot, it is probably going to be the lights, so have backups if possible.

LIGHTING GUIDE AT A GLANCE

Goals (What do you want?)

- View
- Mood
- Depth

Assessment (What do you have?)

- Indoors or out
- Time of day

Plan (What do you need to do?)

- Types of lights
    - Tungsten
    - Halogen
    - Fluorescent
    - LED
- Lighting placement
    - Key light
    - Fill light
    - Rim light
    - Three-point lighting
    - Back light
    - Practicals
- Lighting stands and modifiers
    - Light stands
    - Tripods
    - Diffusers
    - Gels
    - Reflectors

Action (Do it!)

- Setup time
- Power requirements

2.4: SCENE COMPOSITION

Loud DOGS ARE BY My Door

Scene composition

When we talk about scene composition, we are talking about what the viewer sees inside the rectangle of vision that we call the screen.

> FOR ME, SETTING UP SHOTS PROPERLY CONTINUES TO BE THE TOUGHEST PART. PARTICULARLY ON A LIMITED BUDGET AND TIME FRAME, MAKING SURE IT'S FRAMED AND LIT PROPERLY AND THAT YOUR CAMERA SETTINGS ARE ALL CORRECT IS SO IMPORTANT. SOMETIMES I'LL FORGET SOMETHING SMALL IN THE MOMENT THAT TURNS INTO A BIG PAIN LATER ON.
>
> *—Shaudi Bianca Vahdat, American/Iranian Musician and Theatre Artist*

Scene composition can be thought of in terms of three main components: **Distance**, **Angle**, and **Balance** (the "**DAB**" part of **LDABMD**, *Loud Dogs Are By My Door*.) We'll look at how each part can play a role in telling the story you want to tell, or creating the audience reaction you're going for.

DISTANCE

Loud DOGS Are By My Door

Distance refers to how far away the camera is from the main subject. That distance determines the vocabulary you use to talk about a shot.

The basic distance definitions include:

- Wide or long shot
- Full shot
- Medium shot
- Close-up
- Extreme close-up

Distance is one of the main scene composition considerations when determining what message the scene should have, or what you want the scene to convey, since different distances give different messages.

Wide or long shot

A wide or long shot shows the big picture. It may be of a mountain landscape, a city skyline, or closer to the main subject, but the person or people in the shot are small relative to the rest of the scene.

Wide shots are good for establishing presence and location. They are often used in the beginning of films or story sections to give the viewer a sense of place, before moving in closer to the characters in a story or performance.

Full shot

A full shot refers to a shot where the height of the actor or actors fills most of the frame from top to bottom. Full shots provide a good observational distance—as if the viewer were a near bystander, watching a scene but not a part of it. They work well for action shots where seeing the actor from head to toe helps the viewer understand the action.

Medium shot

A medium shot is close enough to show the main subject from approximately the waist up. This is a conversational distance, similar to the field of view a person would have if they were conversing with someone. It's a good shot for helping the viewer feel a part of the scene, involved in the action.

Close-up

A classic close-up (CU) is a shot where the actor's face fills the frame from top to bottom. Of course, there can be close-ups of other things besides faces, but the distance would be similar to that of a full-face shot, as if you (the viewer) were a few inches away from the subject.

A close-up is an intimate shot. It mimics the scene we would have in our field of vision if we were very close to the subject, which typically would happen if we were in love with the subject or perhaps enraged; in either case, deep emotions are involved.

The close-up reveals the detail of the subject's face, and typically allows for only a single actor in the scene. Close-ups are good for establishing connection and for revealing emotion, since most of our emotional cues come from faces.

Extreme close-up

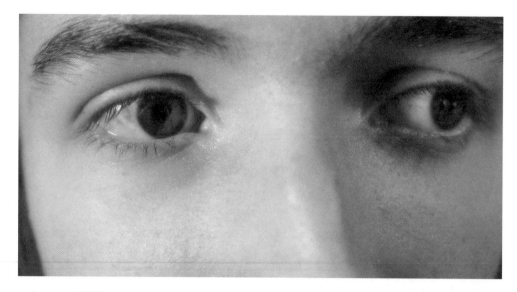

The extreme close-up (ECU) gets even closer, providing even more intimacy and detail. ECUs can focus on some facial feature, particularly those showing the most emotion (often eyes or mouth), but can also refer to anything where the viewer sees much more detail (and less breadth) than normal.

ANGLE

Loud Dogs ARE By My Door

Angle is another scene dimension that can help convey a certain message to the viewer. Angle refers to the slope (angle) of the camera view in relation to the scene.

There are lots of camera angles, but the most basic ones include:

- Eye level
- High (angled down)
- Low (angled up)
- Overhead or bird's eye (pointing straight down)
- Ground level
- Tilted or Dutch angle

The first three are the most common angles a person experiences in daily conversation. The others lend a more unusual perspective to a scene.

Eye level

Eye level is the most common angle, since it equals what we would see looking at another person of roughly the same height. For amateur filmmakers, it is the result of the most conventional way to film, holding a camera up to eye level and pointing the camera toward the face of another person.

As such, eye level represents normalcy and equality. It's the angle for everyday life. It can be effective if that is what you want to represent, but because it's the most familiar, other angles will help add creativity to your scenes and may provide other layers of meaning.

High (angled down)

A high angle, angled down at the subject, indicates that the viewer is in a position of power relative to the subject.

In normal life, we look down at things that are smaller and typically less powerful than we are, particularly children. Bigger things are stronger (and often scarier) than smaller things, and a high angle emphasizes a size difference.

High shots, angled down, are effective at showing a person as lacking strength. If you want to emphasize sickness, uncertainty, or youth, high-angle shots work well. In a music video, a high angle can help to convey the emotion of a weak or troubled subject, whether it be the performer or the protagonist of the story told by the song.

Low (Angled Up)

The low shot, angled up, has the opposite effect of the high shot. In this case, the subject has authority over a weaker audience. Whether showing a monster destroying a city or a performer dominating a concert, angling the camera up is effective at emphasizing a powerful subject.

Overhead or Bird's Eye

The overhead shot, also known as the bird's eye shot (what a bird would see), gives an unusual and unique perspective to a scene. It's not a view people generally have, unless they're on a tall building or looking over the side of a bridge.

What it signifies depends on the circumstance. It can mean detachment from the situation: You (the audience) are not directly involved, you're just passing by overhead. It can also represent omniscience—a god's-eye view. It can provide a good overview of a situation, giving the audience more information and special insight than they normally would expect to have.

Besides being difficult to film (without a drone or a crane), overhead shots should be considered and used carefully so as not to confuse the audience. They can be great shots, but shouldn't be thrown in at random, unless random is really what you're going for.

Ground Level

A ground-level shot is another angle that you wouldn't normally encounter. Ground-level shots can be used to show a secret world not noticed by others, or a weakened view of someone sick or knocked down.

Tilted or Dutch Angle

A tilted or dutch angle shows a scene tilted at approximately 45 degrees. This communicates to the audience that things are off-balance, that something is wrong or in a state of change.

BALANCE

Loud Dogs Are BY My Door

The balance of a scene can help it feel settled or unsettled, calm or chaotic.

Among the many different ways to balance a scene, we'll consider two of the most common: horizontal symmetry and "rule of thirds." We'll also look at why you would want a scene to be purposely off-balance.

Horizontal Symmetry

Horizontal symmetry, where a scene is balanced from side to side, is one of the most basic balances in nature. Symmetry is exhibited by human faces and bodies, as well as many plants and animals, and it naturally feels settled and calm.

Setting up a scene with horizontal symmetry give the scene a solid foundation, making it stable. Symmetry can be strict, where the left and right sides of the frame are a mirror image of each other, or more subtle, with a neutral background and the same number and size of subjects on each side of the frame.

Symmetry is always safe, but it can feel too calm and even boring, depending on the situation or the song, or if used too much. It may be hard for symmetry to feel exciting, but it's hard to go very wrong with horizontal symmetry.

Rule of Thirds

The "rule of thirds" is best described using the illustration below:

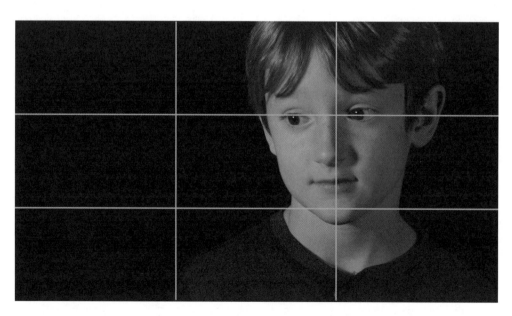

If you divide a rectangle into thirds, horizontally and vertically, you get good guidelines for where the main focus of the scene should be. In particular, the intersection of the upper line with the right or left vertical lines is a good place for the key part of the scene, such as a person's face. Also, if you have a vertical element along one of the vertical lines, or a horizontal element (such as the horizon line in a wide shot) along one of the horizontal lines, the scene will have a good sense of balance.

A rule-of-thirds shot is more dynamic than a symmetrical shot, but it still has naturally comfortable composure to it. If you're unsure of how to balance a shot but don't want the static feel of symmetry, following the rule of thirds is a good way to go.

Off Balance

What if you don't want a comfortable, balanced shot? Off-balance shots are useful in conveying tension, drama, or mystery. When the main subject is near an edge or a corner, and particularly if there is an indication of something important going on outside the frame, it can leave an unsettled feeling in your viewers, which may be just what you want.

Below are some examples of off-balance shots. In each case, the placement and direction of the main subject adds uncertainty to the scene—something is hidden, or something is happening or about to happen that you can't see.

SCENE COMPOSITION AT A GLANCE

Distance

- Wide or long shot
- Full shot
- Medium shot
- Close-up
- Extreme close-up

Angle

- Eye level
- High
- Low
- Overhead
- Ground level
- Tilted

Balance

- Horizontal symmetry
- Rule of thirds
- Off balance

2.5: CAMERA MOVEMENT

Loud Dogs Are By MY Door

Camera movement

GOALS

There are a couple of standard objectives for camera movement during the filming of a video:

1. Moving the camera smoothly (or as smoothly as you want)

2. Moving the camera effectively so your story comes through

Smooth camera movement is a matter of technique, as well as having the right equipment. You can move a camera smoothly without any equipment, but it's a lot harder to do well.

Effective camera movement depends on using the techniques that will best tell your story. Even if you aren't doing a narrative video, it's helpful to know how different movements are typically used and what they might convey to the audience. We'll talk about those more below.

USING TRIPODS

If you want to move the camera while attached to a tripod, the two basic moves are pans and tilts. Panning is rotating the camera horizontally and tilting is rotating the camera vertically.

Note that when your camera is attached to a tripod, the handle for panning and tilting the head should be pointing opposite the direction of the camera—not to the side or the same way as the camera.

Pans

A pan is a good method for following action that happens in a straight line, perpendicular to the movement of the camera (or circling around the camera). Pans are also good for surveying a wide landscape or for moving from one character to another in a scene. A "whip pan" moves the camera rapidly from one part of the scene to the next (or even as a transition between scenes) in a way that jerks the viewers' attention or provides a burst of energy to the narrative.

Here are a few tricks for making your pans as smooth as possible:

- Use a tripod with a fluid head. The mechanism that moves in the head is lubricated with a fluid that helps to smooth out the movements. Cheaper tripod heads have metal moving against metal or plastic against plastic, which won't be nearly as smooth. Of course, fluid heads will cost more.

- Add resistance to the tripod movement. More expensive fluid heads often let you turn a dial that makes the tripod head a little harder to move. This resistance, without locking the tripod head completely, helps create a smoother pan.

- Begin at the end. That is, rotate your camera to what you anticipate will be the end of your shot; align your body so you are comfortable in that position. Then, without moving your feet, rotate the camera to the starting point. Your body may start in a somewhat awkward position, but gradually will shift to a more comfortable stance, which allows you to move the camera smoothly. Though it's more intuitive to start at the beginning, your body would be at its most awkward and twisted at the end of the pan. This may result in some jerkiness at the end.

- Use one finger. Hooking your finger around the tripod handle and slowly pulling the handle toward you should result in a smoother pan than if you grab it with your entire hand and push or pull it.

- If you are not following specific action or doing a whip pan, pan more slowly than you think you need to. Try to take two or three seconds for each 90 degrees of panning. It will seem very slow, but it will make for a smoother shot.

Tilts

Most of the suggestions for pans apply to tilts as well, except that you are moving the camera up and down. Using a fluid head with resistance, finding your end position first, moving slowly, and pushing or pulling lightly rather than firmly gripping the handle will help give you smoother tilts.

A tilt shot is effective for emphasizing the large size of something (starting at the bottom and slowly tilting upward), or going in reverse, showing how small something is by slowing tilting down to it. You can also use a tilt to change the emphasis from things happening on the ground and things happening up in the sky, or the reverse.

MONOPODS

A monopod is like a tripod, but with only one leg; it can help in steadying shots where a tripod isn't available or practical. All monopods allow you to do pans just by twisting or to do tilts by leaning the monopod forward and back. They can also be useful for a DIY approach to some of the other camera moves described below.

DOLLIES, TRUCKS, AND CRANES

Dollies

A dolly is a cart on wheels for moving a camera forward and back, toward or away from a scene. "Dolly" also refers to the action of moving forward or backward. On a movie set, the dolly usually rolls on a special track to make the move as smooth as possible. Typically, the cart provides enough room for the camera operator to stand or sit with the camera on a tripod, and the cart is moved by one or more crew members.

For a DIY shoot, you are unlikely to use a real dolly setup, but if you have a smooth floor or other surface, you can get creative, looking for something with wheels that could be used for dolly shots. For example, wheeled office chairs or utility carts on wheels could work. A bicycle could also be used, assuming you have one person to sit with the camera and at least two people to move the bicycle safely, steadying it and the rider.

You can also do a sort-of mini-dolly shot with a tripod, having just two of the legs extended. Using this method, you slowly tilt the entire tripod (or bipod at this point) forward or back while counter-tilting the tripod head to keep focused on your subject. (This will be clearer by watching the Camera Movement instructional video.)

A dolly shot is effective for increasing the tension and intimacy of a scene by moving closer to it, or doing the opposite by moving away. It can also reveal more detail moving in, or show the larger context by moving out.

Trucks

A "truck" move would also typically be on a cart, but moving side to side, perpendicular to the scene. Trucks are similar to pans in that they can move from one part of a scene to another, or follow action that is moving horizontally in front of the camera.

For small movements, you can use a "slider," which is a rail that attaches to your tripod or sits on a flat surface. Your camera sits on a tripod head or directly on a small stand with small wheels that fit into the rail. A slider allows you to slide your camera smoothly from side to side (or potentially forward and back, or even up and down). It is much less expensive than a truck setup, but because it typically is only about one yard (one meter) long or less, a slider is best for small, subtle movements, or for subjects fairly close to the camera.

The DIY options for truck shots are similar to dolly shots. Also, filming out the window of a car as it drives slowly by your scene could be another option.

Cranes

A crane (or boom or jib) is usually a long pole or mechanical arm secured at one end, with a camera on the other end. This equipment is used for a variety of unique shots: moving overhead, arching over a scene, or moving in multiple directions at once, such as up and over. The largest cranes also have a platform for the camera operator at the end, while smaller ones allow for remote camera control, either mechanically or electronically.

A crane shot can give a wonderfully unique perspective to a scene, but it requires more complicated equipment and is difficult to execute well. You can try a simplified DIY crane shot by attaching your camera (very securely) to the end of an extended monopod (or tripod, if it's light enough), adjusting the camera angle, and focusing at the distance you think you will need. Hold the monopod with the bottom end braced against you and with your two hands on the pole to steady it, lifting it over your head to point down at your scene. This can be somewhat awkward and heavy (you'll be surprised at how quickly your arms tire in this position), and you risk damaging your camera if you aren't completely in control, but it is a quick way to get a unique shot. Try it out ahead of time, and have someone next to you to help control it.

WHAT ABOUT ZOOM?

At first glance, a zoom shot (magnifying a shot by using the zoom feature of your zoom lens) may seem to be as good as a dolly shot and a lot easier. You can attach your camera firmly to a tripod, then all you have to worry about is smoothly rotating the zoom ring to get closer to or further from your subject.

In terms of shot variety, a zoom shot is never as good as a dolly shot. A zoom shot just makes a smaller part of the same shot bigger, rather than really moving closer to the scene, which gives you a different perspective and field of view. If you want to have a close-up or otherwise move into a scene, physically moving the camera closer is always preferable.

WANDERING AROUND

If you want the smoothest "untethered" movements (not connected to a tripod, track, or wheeled dolly) while following a subject or surveying a scene, the easiest but most expensive option is to get a motorized, battery-powered gimbal. A gimbal typically uses three internal motors and software to give the smoothest possible movement to any normal camera actions, so you can walk normally and film with no bouncy or jittery movements.

The price of gimbals continues to fall, and they are less expensive for smaller cameras, so they might be in your budget, particularly as a rental. If you can't afford one, there are other, non-electric camera stabilizers, such as a Steadicam™ or similar devices. They generally cost less than gimbals, but they require more practice and expertise to operate steadily.

At an even more DIY level, you can stabilize camera movements to a certain extent by attaching a tripod, monopod, or something similar to your hand-held camera, and by moving carefully to smooth out movements. The added weight and lower center of gravity will help in this regard. You may have the legs contracted all or part of the way, depending on what balances better. Extending the legs puts the weight lower, but at some point, you risk having the legs bump the ground, so you will want to experiment to find what works best.

Of course, the heavier the camera, the harder it is to carry and the more tired you will get carrying it, so you need to find a happy medium. Even so, a little more effort can be worth it.

In terms of moving carefully, plan to step and shift your weight in such a way that you minimize the natural bounce that happens when you walk. This requires bending both legs and trying to glide smoothly forward as you walk, using a deliberate "heel/toe" motion with each step. (If you have dance training, it will help.) Yes, you will look strange, but it makes a difference.

Finally, if your camera or your lens has automatic stabilization, be sure it is activated when you use hand-held camera movements—unless you purposely want a "shaky cam" look.

I had a student in one of my classes who wanted to make a video for a frantic head-banger rock song, so he wanted to do handheld—the shakier, the better. Near campus, there were some large inflated clear plastic bubbles floating on a reflecting pool that tourists could rent for five minutes to bounce around inside on the surface of the water. He took an action camera into one of the bubbles and recorded a three-minute video selfie of him thrashing around inside the bubble while singing his song. It was anything but smooth, but it worked perfectly for the video.

DRONES

Drones, or, more accurately, motorized remote-control multicopters with attached cameras, are becoming increasingly common and affordable, and they allow all sorts of amazing, well-ordered camera moves in the hands of a skilled operator.

A good "prosumer" video drone comes with a reasonably good camera, a stabilizing gimbal, and full pan and tilt capability. In the right conditions, a good drone can do just about anything we have discussed so far: pan, tilt, truck, dolly, crane, and wander around, along with amazing aerial shots and action-tracking shots over large distances.

Investing in a good drone might seem to be all you would need for creating your moving shots. That's possible, but they have a few big limitations.

- They are more complicated and need more skill to operate effectively.
- They have a short operating time, typically less than 30 minutes for one battery.
- They can't be used in many conditions and locations, including (usually) indoors, outside with high winds, near airports, etc.
- Their use is increasingly restricted and controlled by governments and aviation administrations.
- They are much less robust than other equipment, and when they crash, which is highly likely at some point, they will probably become useless.

Even so, as long as you are aware of the limitations, a drone can be a great option for moving shots.

CAMERA MOVEMENT AT A GLANCE

Goals
- Smooth moves
- Moves to tell your story

Tripods
- Pans
- Tilts

Monopods

Dollies, trucks, and cranes

Zoom?

Wandering around

Drones

2.6: DEPTH OF FIELD

Loud Dogs Are By My DOOR

After considering lighting, distance, angle, balance, and movement, one last thing to concern yourself with is depth of field. That is, how much of your shot do you want to be in sharp focus, and do you want any of it to be blurry?

This artistic decision is a simple part of scene creation with a big impact on how your video is received. In particular, a shallow depth of field (where appropriate) will help make your video look more cinematic and professional, partly because only higher-end video cameras can give you a true shallow depth-of-field, where only part of the image is in focus and the rest is blurred.

WHERE WOULD YOU USE IT?

Shallow depth of field, where only part of the image is in focus, works very well when the subject you want the audience to focus on is in one area of the scene. The most common example in music videos is a single performer, singing or playing to the camera.

If you want the audience to make the strongest connection with the performer, it makes sense to have only the performer in focus so the viewers aren't distracted by anything that is happening in the background. This isn't always your priority—often you will want the entire scene in focus to connect the performer with their environment—but for certain moments of emphasis, this technique can be quite effective.

Shallow depth of field also lets you change a scene significantly just by altering the focus during the shot from something closer to something further away, or vice versa (called "rack focus").

From a DIY perspective, you don't always get to film in the perfect environment (since you may have to take what you can get), so being able to blur out distracting clutter or other details in the background can be a big advantage.

HOW DO YOU GET IT?

A shallow depth of field is possible by using a lens with a low f-stop setting. We go into lots of detail about f-stops in the camera settings chapter, but basically, if you can set your camera lens to an f-stop of 2.8 or lower (2.0, 1.8, or 1.4), it will allow you to get a shallow depth of field. Lenses with this capability are more expensive than the basic "kit" lenses that come with DSLRs and similar cameras, so they would typically be an extra purchase or rental.

2.7: SETTING UP THE CAMERA

Could Loud Bulls Torment Me More?

LOUD BULLS

Once you have decided how to create your scenes, you need to make sure your camera has all of the necessary parts and pieces so it will do what you want. This section is most relevant for DSLR or high-end mirrorless cameras, since those cameras have the most "bang for the buck" for DIY filmmakers. Even so, the information could be useful for other types of cameras as well.

> IT'S HARD TO REMEMBER ALL THE PREP WORK: CHARGING BATTERIES, GATHERING EQUIPMENT, ADJUSTING THE CAMERA SETTINGS, SETTING UP LIGHTING, SETTING UP THE SCENE, ETC. IT'S EASY TO GET SO EXCITED TO START FILMING AND MISS THE STEPS IT TAKES TO GET THE BEST QUALITY FOOTAGE.
>
> *—Savannah Philyaw, Indie-Folk Singer-Songwriter*

Loud Bulls will help remind you about the steps to take, in order, to get your camera ready to go:

Could	Card (memory)
Loud	Lens
Bulls	Battery
Torment	Tripod plate
Me	Manual control
More	Manual focus

CARD

COULD Loud Bulls Torment Me More

In terms of the physical setup of the camera, inserting the memory card is one of the first things to do.

Video takes up a lot of space. How much space will depend on the file format your camera records in, but filming a full music video with multiple takes can easily fill up the available memory. Since space is so critical to your filming experience (without memory for your digital recording, there will be no video), getting this one thing wrong can wipe out all the other things you do correctly. So let's look carefully at how to get it right.

Most cameras use a removable card, often an SD or micro-SD card, to store the video. If you're filming with your phone and it has a removable card, having extra cards will help you have the space you need. If you're filming using built-in, non-expandable memory, the space will fill remarkably fast. If you're filming in high-definition (HD, sometimes called 1080), or even 4K (which takes up four times as much space as HD), you may be out of space in minutes, which could wreak havoc with your day of filming.

If you're using memory cards, there might be other things on the cards—other videos, photos, or even backup files from your computer—maybe things you don't even realize are there. (I speak from experience, especially the experience of my students.) Simply put, you may have a lot less space than you think, and are likely to run out of room long before you want to be done filming.

Figure out how much space you think you'll need—do some test filming to see how big the file gets. If you want to be on the safe side, estimate what you'll need, then double it.

Try to have empty, newly formatted cards if at all possible—and format the cards in the camera you will use, to ensure that there won't be problems recording to the card.

Also, try to have at least two cards for each camera—for backup, and just in case one of the cards is bad (which happens).

LENS

Could LOUD Bulls Torment Me More

Once you have an empty, freshly formatted card in the camera, a next logical step is to make sure the right lens for your shot is attached to the camera. The chapter on choosing a camera has some guidelines about which lens to use.

BATTERY

Could Loud BULLS Torment Me More

If you have a camera with a removable battery, the next step is to insert the battery. Turn on the camera and check the battery meter to make sure your battery is fully charged. If it's not, and you have others, this is the time to put in a fresh battery.

If your camera (such as your phone) doesn't have a removable battery, check to see how much charge you have available. Ideally, you will have charged your battery fully before getting to this point, but if the battery is lower than you expect, do something about it so you're not stuck with a dead battery in the middle of a shoot.

Portable external batteries can be a good investment if you plan to do a lot of filming with your phone.

TRIPOD PLATE

Could Loud Bulls TORMENT Me More

If you are using a tripod (a good idea most of the time) and the tripod has a removable plate that can be attached to the camera (all but the cheapest tripods do), now is the time to put on the tripod plate. The reason for not doing it earlier is in case the tripod plate would block the access door for the removable battery. Most interchange-able-lens cameras have battery access through the bottom of the camera, right next to the tripod mounting hole; if you put on the tripod plate before putting in the battery, you'll just have to take it off again. (Speaking from experience....)

Make sure the tripod plate is attached tightly and securely, since that connection may be the main thing keeping your camera from crashing to the ground. You may have to tighten the tripod plate screw with a small coin or something similar. It's handy to keep a metal washer—a small metal circle with a hole in it—on a string attached to your tripod so you can tighten the plate whenever you need to.

MANUAL CONTROL

Could Loud Bulls Torment ME More

If your camera has the option for manual control—meaning you will set the f-stop, shutter speed, ISO, etc.—typically you will want to use it. On many interchangeable lens cameras, there is a dial at the top with various options; turn the dial to "M" for manual control or whatever setting gives you the most control during filmmaking.

A fully automatic camera—including most phones and many action cams—won't have a manual option and will choose the exposure combination it thinks will give the best image. Nevertheless, there are many reasons and situations for wanting to control them yourself. The next chapter in this section will teach you what you need to know about each of the settings, so you can control them to get the image you want.

MANUAL FOCUS

Could Loud Bulls Torment Me MORE

Manual focus gives you more control over the image so you can get just the one you want. Many automatic cameras won't offer the option, but if it's possible to set the focus to manual, usually from a dial on top of the camera or a switch on the side of the lens, be certain you are set for manual now.

Manual focus is most important when you have shallow depth of field—so only a small part of the image will be in focus—or when you have a lot of movement in the scene, as when there are some people in front, some behind, and lots of movement.

Automatic focus tries to figure out what you want to focus on, and gives you what it thinks you want, but it doesn't always get it right. In particular, many automatic focus systems look for faces in the scene, but if you have faces at different distances from the camera, there will be problems.

There are some high-end cameras with excellent auto focus, allowing you to track a particular person regardless of the distance they are from the camera. If you are moving around and have that kind of focus, it can be useful, but be sure to test it first. You don't want the scene to be ruined by autofocus searching (going in and out of focus as the camera tries to figure out what is important).

Some cameras (such as action cameras) have a fixed focus, meaning there is no option to change the focus. The camera settings try to get everything in focus, which avoids some problems, but also takes away flexibility, so it's not ideal except in high-action situations where your subject is constantly moving and could be any distance from the camera.

CAMERA SETUP AT A GLANCE

Card (empty, with spares)

Lens

Battery (charged, with spares)

Tripod plate

Manual control

Manual focus

2.8: ADJUSTING THE CAMERA SETTINGS

Maybe Someone Will Fix It For

Understanding f-stop

If you are using a DSLR or mirrorless camera for creating videos, you should have the ability to take total control over the settings of your camera. Although the camera may also have an automatic mode, similar to what you would have on your phone, in most cases understanding and controlling the various camera settings and options will give you the most control over your finished video. Even if you plan to film with a fully automatic camera, this section will help you understand what each setting is for.

It's hard to avoid getting fairly technical in this chapter, but the most technical parts are separated into clearly marked "geeky details" sections, which will be helpful for reference.

> DON'T LOSE THE BIG PICTURE WHILE DEALING WITH TECHNICAL ISSUES. THAT IS THE HARDEST THING TO REMEMBER WHILE MAKING A MUSIC VIDEO.
>
> *—Kasia Kijek and Przemek Adamski, Polish Film Directors and Animators*

If you want to skip to the end of the chapter ("Camera settings at a glance" and "Scenarios"), you can get the shorthand version, and then work backward for anything you need more detail on.

Camera settings are represented in the third stanza of the "Loud dogs" poem:

Maybe	Movie size
Someone	Shutter speed
Will	White balance
Fix	F-stop
It	ISO
For	Focus

(The last word in the poem, "**Me**," stands for "Movie time!")

MOVIE SIZE

MAYBE Someone Will Fix It For

Movie size may be called different things by different manufacturers, but it refers to the combination of frame resolution and frame rate. Although they are two separate concepts and specifications, they are usually dealt with together, and camera options usually present them in pairs, for technical reasons that we'll get into a little later.

Resolution

Resolution in digital cameras refers to the number of pixels being recorded on the camera's sensor. Terms such as "HD," "1080p," and "4K" refer to resolution.

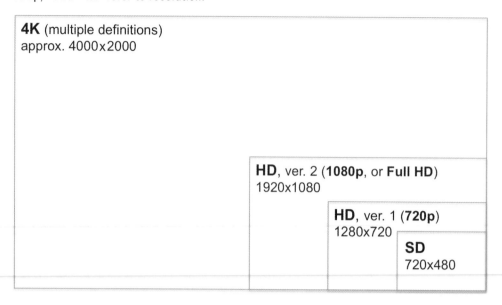

For example, "HD" (High Definition) is an industry and marketing term that was created to distinguish higher-definition cameras and screen from "SD" (Standard Definition), which was the TV broadcast and DVD standard for many years. An SD sensor records video at 720 pixels wide (horizontally) by 480 pixels tall (vertically) (or 576 pixels, depending on the region you are in), to play back on an SD screen. In other words, SD is 720x480 or 720x576.

HD can refer to either "720" (1280x720) or "1080" (1920x1080). Setting standards requires getting everyone to agree, and they usually don't (VHS vs. Betamax, six different regional DVD formats, etc.), which is why there are two specifications for HD. For this "standard," the single number refers to the number of pixels vertically on the camera sensor or on the display screen. As shown in the example above, 1080 HD has over four times the resolution of SD (or DVD) because it is more than twice as high and twice as wide. (720x480 = 346K pixels, 1920x1080 = 2,074K pixels.)

In practical terms, higher resolution usually means a better picture, since you are less likely to notice the pixels or individual dots of color in the image.

1080p or 1080i? (Geeky details)

Either 720 HD or 1080 HD can be "i" or "p," with "i" referring to interlacing (the way broadcast televisions used to display video) and "p" referring to "progressive" (the way computers and modern televisions display it). Interlacing was necessary because of the technical limitations of early systems, but progressive is preferred and used in all modern systems, so "1080" will typically be "1080p."

If you have older footage, it may use "i" (interlacing), which is important only if there are synchronization problems while editing. You will know if you have interlacing sync issues because your video will have "combing" problems. If such is the case, do some digging to figure out how to fix it, since it's an obscure problem, but "interlaced combing" is a term to include in your research.

4K (or 6K, 8K, etc.)

A more recent "standard" is "4K" video, which is approximately four times the resolution of 1080. As with many standards, there isn't complete agreement on what the standard is, so "4K" may refer to any one of three different resolutions, either 3840 pixels or 4096 horizontally and different pixel counts vertically. In general terms, 4K refers to the number of horizontal pixels in the frame—as opposed to 1080 or 720, which refers to the vertical number. (In "4K talk," 1080p would be "2K.")

6K and 8K are emerging standards, also referring to the approximate number of horizontal pixels on a sensor or screen. It remains to be seen whether these formats really provide better pictures, or are primarily a way for manufacturers to sell more screens. (At some point, depending on the overall size of the screen, the dots are so small and so close together that our eyes really can't distinguish the difference.)

Resolution: What matters

As a music video producer, there are a few important things to remember about film resolution:

- Higher resolution in any given camera usually means a higher quality picture, since most cameras offer a variety of resolution options.

- Because of that, in general, you should use the highest resolution available on whatever camera you have. If you need to take video with your phone camera, check the settings to make sure the resolution is as high as it can go.

- If your resolution is higher than you need for the final product, you can always reduce the resolution with no loss of quality. Increasing resolution ("upsizing") will decrease the quality.

- The cost of high-resolution video is much larger file sizes (for example, 4K is four times larger than 1080) and potentially more difficulty editing if your computer doesn't have sufficient memory or storage space for the larger file sizes.

- Practically speaking, a very high resolution on a small screen makes very little difference. 4K in a movie theater is a significant improvement over 1080p, but 4K for a video that will be watched on a phone might be overkill.

- A camera usually offers a lower resolution option along with a higher frame rate, so if you need the higher frame rate (for example, for creating slow motion in post production), you may need to choose a lower resolution.

Frame Rates

The discussion about frame rates also diverges into a discussion about standards, or lack of standards. There are three fairly standard frame rates (measured in frames per second, or fps) that are quite similar but not exactly the same: 24, 25, and 30. This means that the video records and shows either 24, 25, or 30 still frames in succession every second. (Remember that "movies" are just a bunch of still photos, each slightly different than the previous one and shown so quickly that it looks like smooth movement.)

Really 24? (Geeky details)

In fact, the 24 fps standard is really 23.976 fps, and 30 fps is really 29.97 fps. To further muddy the waters, some cameras use an actual 24.000 and 30.000 fps rate, although those are the exception. In practice, the editing software usually figures out how to make it all look right.

Frame rates: What matters

The practical differences among the three standard frame rates are these:

- 24 is the "film" standard, that is, most films shown in movie theaters are filmed and shown at 24 fps.

- 25 is the "PAL" broadcast standard, used in Europe and much of the rest of the world, except…

- 30 is the "NTSC" standard, used primarily in the US and Japan.

Filming a video at 24 fps, along with a "180-degree shutter" (a shutter speed that is half the frame rate, discussed later in this chapter), gives a recording a more film-like look because of the motion blur that occurs at this speed. Because of this, many people prefer to film at 24 fps, so this is a good option if it is available to you.

Filming a video at 25 or 30 fps

If you have the choice of filming at 25 or 30 fps, which should you choose?

As mentioned above, 30 is the broadcast standard in the United States and Japan, but 25 is the standard in Europe and other parts of the world. If you are filming for broadcast television with a specific geographic market in mind, it's best to use the standard of that market.

If your end goal is to upload to YouTube or another online platform, it really doesn't matter. Browsers in any country of the world can play online videos filmed at any standard speed, so it won't make a difference.

If you are filming with multiple cameras, it's best to set all cameras to film at the same frame rate. If you have one camera that does only one rate and the others can do more than one, choose the rate common to all cameras.

Flickering problem? (Geeky details)

There is one circumstance where the frame rate really does matter, and that's in certain situations when filming with artificial lights (such as indoor overhead lights).

In some cases, you might notice that your footage flickers, with slight dark and light horizontal bands alternating on the screen. One possible reason for this is related to why the U.S. and European standards are different.

In NTSC countries such as the U.S., electricity is produced at 60 hertz, which means the current alternates (the A of AC) 60 times every second. In PAL countries, the electricity is produced at 50 Hz. For certain types of lights, this current alteration means the lights actually flicker at that speed; for example, 50 times per second. Because it is faster than our eyes detect, we never normally notice it.

If your filming frame rate is synchronized with the AC rate (30 fps for 60 Hz or 25 fps for 50 Hz), the camera shouldn't notice it either. If you have a flickering light and are at the wrong frame rate (such as 30 fps with 50 Hz AC), the flickers won't synchronize with the frames, and you may get some flickering.

If that is the case, try changing your frame rate, or try to find a different light source that doesn't flicker.

What about higher frame rates?

As we will talk about in the chapter on time remapping, higher frame rates are useful for filming in slow motion. If you want to slow something to half speed, the best way is to film at double the frame rate, then "recharacterize" the footage in post-production to the normal frame rate.

For example, you've determined that you want to produce your video at 30 frames per second. You also want a section of it to be in slow motion, at 50 percent of the normal speed. If you film those sections at 60 fps, recharacterize them in post to 30 fps; then, everything will be going at half speed.

We talk more about the details in the later chapter. Just recognize that a higher frame rate on any given camera usually has a cost, since the processing on the computer that is in your camera has to deal with both frame rate and resolution at the same time. Faster frame rate means less time to deal with the number of pixels, so the resolution (number of pixels) is usually lower.

Some cameras offer very high frame rates, but with resolutions that are so low they are unusable for all practical purposes. (Remember that lower resolution means less detail and clarity.) For example, if your camera gives you 240 fps, but at 480 resolution (true of some action cameras), you probably won't want to use it unless you are purposefully going for a lo-fi, old-school look in your video.

Movie Size summary

Whatever combination of resolution and frame rate you decide on, you typically have to make that decision only once for a given video. The exception is if you are shooting some scenes in slow motion, in which case you will have multiple frame rates for one production. If possible, all cameras used for the video should be set for the same movie size. If they can't be, the editing software can compensate for the differences, but the end product will be better if it doesn't have to.

SHUTTER SPEED

Maybe SOMEONE Will Fix It For

Once you decide on your movie size, the next thing to set is the shutter speed.

In regular photography, shutter speed is a more complicated topic, since you can vary shutter speed from quite slow (multiple seconds or even minutes per shot) to very fast (thousandths of a second), and which speed you use depends on the results you want.

The movie standard

For video and film, the issue is usually a lot simpler. Thanks to the long-standing tradition of the movie industry, which specifies 24 fps for the frame rate (since that's what people are used to), the traditional shutter speed is essentially half the frame rate. So, for 24 fps, where each frame is 1/24th of a second, you would use a shutter speed of 1/48th of a second (often displayed on cameras as just "48.")

180-degree shutter (Geeky details)

In traditional filmmaking, this is referred to as a "180-degree shutter," since the original shutters for movie cameras were rotating disks, with half of the disk (180 out of 360 degrees) open and the other half closed. Since the disk rotates once per frame, 24 times per second, the exposure is equivalent to half of that time, or 1/48th of a second.

Using this rule, if you are filming at 25 fps, the shutter speed will be 1/50th of a second, and 30 fps will be 1/60th. In practice, your camera may not have all the shutter speeds that correspond to exactly half of all the frame rates it offers, so you choose the closest one. For example, your camera may let you film at 24 or 25 fps, but it offers only 1/50th, not 1/48th, of a second for shutter speed. The slight difference shouldn't really matter.

Other options

Do you have to film at that shutter speed? No, but filming at the movie standard will make moving objects blur in a way that people are used to.

Too slow a shutter speed will create more blur, making the footage look mushy. Too fast will make it seem too "sharp"—more like a video game, which typically uses the equivalent of faster shutter speeds.

If you want more or less blur, you can choose different shutter speeds, up to a point. If you are filming at 24 fps—that is, if you're taking a new image every 1/24th of a second—then it is physically impossible to have a shutter speed slower than 1/24th of second. However, you can make your shutter speed faster, up to the limits of the camera. Faster shutter speeds will make the action crisper with less or no blur (as mentioned above, more like a video game).

Shutter speed summary

Similar to movie size, you typically will make your shutter speed decision just once for a video (unlike some of the later settings, which are changed more frequently). Whether you want traditional movie blur or something different, try to adjust all the cameras on your shoot so they have the same setting.

A note about the exposure trio: shutter speed, f-stop, ISO

We've had an entire chapter about lighting, which you know is critical to making a good image.

When it comes to recording the light onto your film (or onto your digital sensor), there are three key factors: shutter speed, f-stop or aperture, and ISO. We'll talk about f-stop and ISO later in this chapter, but in terms of light, it's helpful to consider all three at the same time, since they all affect how much light is recorded by the camera sensor.

- **Shutter speed** affects how blurry a moving image is, but it also affects how much light gets to the image. A slower shutter speed = more light (and more blur).

- **F-stop**, which is a measure of the aperture or size of the lens opening, affects the depth of field of an image, but also how much light gets to the sensor. Lower f-stop = larger aperture = more light (and shallower depth of field).

- **ISO** is a measure of the sensitivity of the sensor to light, or how quickly it can process light and color information for the image. A higher ISO = faster light processing (and more digital noise, which we'll talk about later).

In terms of our shutter-speed discussion: If, for example, you want less blur so you increase the shutter speed, that will leave less time for light to be recorded on the camera sensor. To have a proper exposure, you will have to compensate by lowering the f-stop and/or increasing the ISO, although doing each of these will have other consequences (shallower depth of field, and more digital noise, respectively).

The automatic settings on your cameras and cell phones make all those decisions for you. They figure out what they think is the best combination of shutter speed, f-stop, and ISO for a given exposure. If you want to control the amount of blur, or the depth of field, or even the image quality, it's best to set those options manually.

It may seem complicated at this point, but it gets easier with practice, and allows you to create better images and videos.

WHITE BALANCE

Maybe Someone WILL Fix It For

Once you have set the movie size and the shutter speed, the next setting to check is white balance. This isn't directly related to how much light the camera gets. Instead, it is a setting that defines what "white" means.

As you learned in the Lighting Fundamentals chapter, "white" light isn't really a single white. It has a color temperature that might make it appear more orangish or bluish. As far as the camera is concerned, it wants to know what the color temperature is so it can recreate "white" as accurately as possible (which in turn will achieve the main goal, making the human skin tones look as natural as possible).

Our eyes automatically compensate when we see something white, so we tend not to think of it as a more bluish white or a more orangish white. However, cameras have settings to compensate for different lighting conditions, so white will look more "white" on screen. If they get it wrong, the resulting images have a noticeable blue or orange tint.

As a camera operator, you want to be aware of this. Although cameras with full manual controls usually have a way to specify what the white balance is, they usually also have an "automatic white balance" setting that does a pretty good job.

For many of the cameras I have used and in most lighting situations, the automatic setting is fine, so in this step (after setting movie size and shutter speed), I usually check to make sure the setting is on automatic, and look at the monitor to see that the colors look right.

Sometimes the light will be doing strange things, and you will want to set your white balance manually. This is best done by pointing your camera at something you know is white (or even better, special cards made for the purpose of white balancing) and going through the adjustments, which differ depending on what kind of camera you have.

If the camera white balance was set to manual the last time it was used, then you will want to make sure it is set properly for your current situation, or turn it back to automatic.

Also, recognize that if you change locations during your shoot, for example, going from indoors (with artificial lights that will be one color) to outdoors (with a different color temperature), the white balance will change. Automatic should take care of it, but you'll want to check.

Fix it in post?

If, for some reason, the white balance just wasn't recorded right and your film is all bluish or orangish, can you correct the color in post-production? Unless you have a very high-end camera that shoots in RAW format (which takes up a huge amount of space because it is uncompressed), fixing white balance after shooting is an uncertain proposition. You can fix coloring a little, but if white is off, it's hard to correct. With RAW footage, you can change the white balance in post processing, but most DIYers won't be using cameras that have that capability.

Bottom line: In most cases, make sure white balance is set to automatic, then go on to the next step. As long as the automatic white balance is working well, you need to set it only once during your filming session.

F-STOP

Maybe Someone Will FIX It For

F-stop, also known as aperture, is generally your next concern when setting up your camera. F-stop and aperture aren't really the same thing, but the terms are often used interchangeably.

The aperture of your camera is basically the (adjustable) size of the hole in your lens that lets light through. The way the size of the aperture is indicated to the camera operator is by the f-stop. The f-stop number (N) is actually a ratio: f (the focal length of the lens) divided by D (the diameter of the aperture opening).

There's a reason we use an f-stop number instead of just the size of the aperture. You want to know how much light is getting to the sensor, and the amount of light that gets to the sensor is affected by both the length of the lens (focal length) and the size of the aperture. If you have a longer lens, essentially a longer tunnel for the light to get through, less of it will get to the sensor, so the two are related.

Using an f-number, you can accurately compare how much light is getting to your camera, regardless of which lens you use. For example, if you have a 50mm lens and a 150mm lens, and they are both set to f/4, you know that the same amount of light is getting to the sensor, and images from either lens will be exposed the same.

Big vs. small numbers

On a typical lens, you'll see f-stop numbers like 2.8, 4.0, 5.6, 8.0, and so on. They might go as low as 1.8 or even 1.4, or as high as 22 or more.

$f/2.8$ indicates a larger opening than $f/4.0$—in fact, the aperture of a lens (the area of the hole) at $f/2.8$ is twice as big as the aperture at $f/4.0$, so $f/2.8$ is said to be "one stop brighter" or faster than $f/4.0$, meaning it will let in twice as much light.

The numbers don't go in nice, even increments because they are ratios that deal with the diameter of circles. The f-number (N) $= f/D$, where f is the focal length, and D is the diameter of the aperture.

Math example (Even geekier details)

Since $N = f/D$, then $D = f/N$
- For a 50mm lens, $f = 50$
- If the f-stop (N) $= 1.0$, then $D = 50/1 = 50$mm
- If the f-stop $= 1.4$, then $D = 50/1.4 = 35.7$mm

Since what we're interested in is the comparative area of the circular aperture (how big the hole is):

- Area of a circle $= \pi r^2$, or $\pi(D/2)^2$
- 50mm lens at $f/1.0$: $3.14 * (50/2)^2 = 1964$mm^2
- 50mm lens at $f/1.4$: $3.14 * (35.7/2)^2 = 1002$mm^2

So, the area of the aperture at $f/1.0$ is (roughly) twice as big as the area of the aperture at $f/1.4$, letting in twice as much light, or "one stop" more of light.

What it all means

With f-stops, smaller numbers represent larger apertures and are "brighter," "faster," or let in more light than larger numbers.

If you are in a low-light situation, a smaller f-stop will allow you to get more light to your sensor so you get a better exposure that isn't too dark.

If you are in the bright sunlight, you may need to use a larger f-stop, unless you use a special filter called an "ND filter" to reduce some of the light.

Also, smaller f-stops have a shallower depth of field than larger f-stops.

If you want to focus on the face of an individual singer and blur the background, a small f-stop (2.8 or less) is a good choice.

If you are filming a large concert audience and you want the near and far people to all be in focus, a larger f-stop is required.

Lenses can be set to a variety of f-stops, but more expensive lenses typically have a lower minimum f-stop than cheaper lenses of the same focal length. For example, an expensive lens could have a minimum f-stop of 1.4 or 1.8, whereas a cheaper lens might go down only to $f/4.0$.

While you'll probably plan to set movie size, shutter speed, and white balance only once for your video shoot, you might set a different f-stop for every scene, depending on the lighting and depth of field requirements.

Depth of field vs. the exposure trio

When you set the f-stop of your lens, your main artistic concern should be your depth of field: Do you want a shallow focus, or a deep one? Whatever you pick will affect how much light gets to your sensor. Since you have already set one part of the exposure trio (shutter speed) and are now setting the second (f-stop), if your image still isn't exposed properly (too bright or too dark), the next setting (ISO) will help you get the exposure that you want.

ISO

Maybe Someone Will Fix IT For

The ISO is a number that measures the sensitivity of a film or camera sensor to light. This sensitivity is sometimes referred to as "speed" (ISO 200 is twice as fast as ISO 100).

The higher the number, the faster the film can record light. If all else is equal (referring to the exposure trio, for a given f-stop and shutter speed), a higher ISO will give you a brighter image.

Stops again (Geeky details)

Unlike f-stops, ISO numbers are easy to understand. A doubling of the ISO doubles the amount of light sensitivity. The increments are also referred to as "stops," so ISO 200 is twice as fast as, or one stop faster than, ISO 100; ISO 400 is twice as fast as ISO 200, etc.

With ISO, the higher the number, the more "noise" or color artifacts appear; that's the biggest caveat. Basically, the sensor has to figure out the correct color for each one of its millions of pixels. A higher ISO means it has to work faster and harder, so it gets more of the pixel colors wrong. This results in dots or blotches of incorrect color on your image.

The base or highest quality ISO for most cameras is 100, and as the ISO increases, the quality decreases, but slowly at first. Depending on the camera, ISO of 400, 800, 1600 or even higher might still be perfectly acceptable quality. Nearly every camera has a seriously degraded image as it reaches its maximum possible ISO.

Since ISO is the last part of the exposure trio you adjust, you need to set it high enough to get a good exposure—and you may need to change it for every scene. If that results in an image with a lot of unwanted noise, you have various options. You can back up in the process and see if you can use a wider f-stop (although it will give you a shallower depth of field), or if you can slow the shutter speed (although the movement will be blurrier), or ideally, if you can add more lights to the scene. Adding more lights is the hardest option, but it will give the best results.

FOCUS

Maybe Someone Will Fix It FOR

Focus is the last step before pushing the Record button. Maybe your camera has great automatic focus, even in video mode, and you don't have to worry about this step. But for maximum creative control, you'll want to focus manually if you can, particularly if you're using a shallow depth of field. If there are many things in the scene at different distances from the camera, the camera may not know what to focus on, so doing it manually will give you the best results.

MAKE SURE THE CAMERA IS CONSTANTLY IN FOCUS; THAT'S THE HARDEST THING TO REMEMBER WHILE MAKING A MUSIC VIDEO. EVERY TIME YOU MOVE THE CAMERA, IT HAS TO BE REFOCUSED. THERE IS NOTHING WORSE THAN SHOOTING ALL DAY AND GETTING BLURRY FOOTAGE.

– Spencer Malley, Musician

Some cameras have a temporary zoom or magnification feature to help you with manual focusing; always use it if you can. Also, if a person's face is the most important part of the scene, focus on their eyes, since that will give the best overall impression of clarity.

If you're using auto focus and either the camera or your subjects is moving around a lot, the camera is likely to get confused. But if you have a small monitor, even using manual focus can be difficult while filming. Here are a couple of tips that can help in that situation.

1. Use a smaller f-stop, which will give you a deeper depth of field, so more of the shot will be in focus regardless of where you move.

2. If you need to change the focus during the filming because you are moving closer to or farther from your subject during the shot, figure out exactly where you will start and end, and do a careful focus at each point before you begin to record. With each focus setting, mark the very top of your focus ring using a small piece of tape. During the shot, as you move from the beginning position to the end position, you can rotate your focus ring smoothly from the beginning piece of tape to the end piece, knowing that your focus should be sharp throughout the shot.

The most important rule for focusing: Always do it before you press the Record button. Even if nothing has changed from one shot to the next, checking the focus is a good idea before every shot. You may find the focus of the previous shot wasn't as sharp as you wanted. After taking pains to get the lighting just right and the exposure set exactly how you want it, you can ruin a shot most easily by being out of focus. (Again, speaking from experience....)

CAMERA SETTINGS AT A GLANCE

Movie size

- Resolution
- Frame rate

Shutter speed

White balance

F-stop

ISO

Focus

CAMERA SETTINGS SCENARIOS

Since there are lots of settings to keep track of, here are three scenarios and the settings you might be using for each of them.

Settings	Outside in full sun	In a dark dance club with changing colored lights	Indoors in a recording studio
Movie size: • Resolution • Frame rate	• 1080p or 4K • 24 fps	• 1080p or 4K • 24 fps & 48 or 60 fps for slow-motion footage	• 1080p or 4K • 24 fps
Shutter speed	• 1/50	• 1/50 & 1/100 or 1/120	• 1/50
White balance	• AWB	• Fixed WB (warm or cool) depending on your desired look, since the colored lights could throw off the AWB	• AWB unless the studio has outdoor window light and unmatching indoor bulbs, in which case, experiment with different settings
F-stop	• Fairly high (11+) because of the bright sun	• Lower (<4) would be better with the lower lights but will reduce the depth of field, so depends on the look you want	• Probably 5.6 or lower, depending on the depth of field you want
ISO	• Lowest setting should work	• Will need fairly high setting for the low light	• As low as possible (bring in extra lights if needed)
Focus	• Before every shot	• Before every shot	• Before every shot

2.9: MOVIE TIME!

Maybe Someone Will Fix It For ME!

Now that you understand the preparation steps for producing your video, you're ready to start filming. (In practice, the preparation should take a lot less time than reading all these chapters.)

Some of the challenges and opportunities that happen during filming were discussed in Chapter 1.2 on music video types. This would be a good time to review those, now that you have a more definite idea about what you are going to shoot.

We'll start with some great advice from people with a range of experiences, from making just a few music videos to creating them professionally.

ADVICE FOR PERFORMERS WHO AREN'T DIRECTING

WHEN YOU'RE APPEARING IN A MUSIC VIDEO, ESPECIALLY IF YOU'RE NOT DIRECTING, THE MORE YOU KNOW ABOUT YOURSELF, THE BETTER. DO YOU HAVE A GOOD SIDE? MOST PEOPLE DO. DO YOU HATE WATCHING YOURSELF LOOK DOWN (OR UP) OR AT YOUR INSTRUMENT? DO YOU PREFER TO LOOK DIRECTLY INTO THE CAMERA, OR ABOVE IT, OR OFF TO ONE SIDE OR THE OTHER? DO YOU DO BETTER WITH DIRECT LIGHTING, OR LIGHTING FROM ABOVE OR FROM A CERTAIN ANGLE? THE MORE YOU DO THIS, THE MORE YOU'LL MAKE THESE DISTINCTIONS, AND THEY CAN DEFINITELY SAVE YOU TIME. BE SURE TO DISCUSS THESE THINGS WITH YOUR DIRECTOR DURING THE PLANNING STAGES OF THE SHOOT—DEFINITELY BEFORE THE SETUP. IF YOU HAVE NO IDEA, YOU CAN EXPERIMENT BY SHOOTING YOURSELF ON YOUR PHONE TRYING VARIOUS POSITIONS, LIGHTING, ETC.

– Stephen Webber, Executive Director, BerkleeNYC

I FELT ACTUALLY REALLY COMFORTABLE ON THE SET BECAUSE THE PRESSURE WAS NOT ON ME AS A PERFORMER. THE PRESSURE WAS ON THE MUSIC VIDEO DIRECTOR AND THE CAMERA OPERATORS—I JUST HAD TO JAM OUT AND HAVE FUN AND LET THEM DO THEIR WORK! I REALISED THAT IT TAKES A LOT OF TIME TO PRODUCE A MUSIC VIDEO, SO PATIENCE IS AN IMPORTANT FACTOR FOR THE MUSICIANS. AND IT'S DIFFICULT BECAUSE OVER TIME YOU GET TIRED AND START TO LOSE YOUR SPARK! BUT EACH TIME I HEARD "ACTION," I NEEDED TO PEP UP AND BE ENERGETIC AGAIN, EVEN IF I WASN'T FEELING IT.

—John C. Leavitt, Composer, Arranger, Pianist

ADVICE FOR DIRECTORS WHO AREN'T PERFORMING

WHEN MAKING A MUSIC VIDEO, REMEMBER IT'S ABOUT THE ARTIST AND THE SONG, NOT YOU AND YOUR DESIRE TO MAKE A SHORT FILM/EXPERIMENTAL ART PIECE/VFX REEL/ANY OTHER KIND OF SHOW-OFF SESSION.

—Nick Clark, Film Producer, Director and Editor

ALWAYS KEEP THE SONG IN MIND. YOU ARE NOT DOING YOUR FILM—YOU ARE DOING A FILM FOR A SONG. JUST GIVE LOVE TO ALL THE PEOPLE YOU ARE WORKING WITH AND THEY WILL GIVE THEIR BEST.

—Greg et Lio, French Film Directors and Photographers

EACH ARTIST HAS DIFFERENT VISIONS—SOMETIMES THEY ARE CLEAR AND SOMETIMES THEY'RE SUPER VAGUE. YOU HAVE TO COMMUNICATE WITH THEM AND MAKE SURE THE IMAGE YOU SHOOT/EDIT IS CLOSE TO WHAT THEY ARE LOOKING FOR. IN SOME CASES, YOU NEED TO LEARN TO REJECT THEIR IDEAS IF THEY'RE NOT DOABLE (BUDGET/LOGISTICALLY) AND GIVE THEM BETTER SUGGESTIONS.

—Simon Yu, Musician, Music Video Director

REMEMBER THAT MOST MUSICIANS ARE NOT ACTORS. YOUR BEST DIRECTOR'S HAT MUST BE ON TO EASE THEM INTO SIMPLY BEING THEMSELVES IN FRONT OF A CAMERA.

—Anjie Concepcion, Audio-Visual Artist, Songwriter, Music Video Director

ADVICE FOR EVERYONE ON THE SET

WHEN MAKING A MUSIC VIDEO, BEING POSITIVE AND PROFESSIONAL ABOUT THE WORK AND BELIEVING IN WHAT YOU ARE HOPING TO ACHIEVE HELPS GET THE BEST OUT OF ALL INVOLVED.

—Michael Sean Harris, Jamaican Vocalist, Electronic Musician and Educator

In the planning stage, you worked out scheduling and logistics, and now is the time when it all comes together. You should review (again) what you planned and make sure everyone involved knows where and when to go, and everyone and everything has a way to get there. (Get everyone's contact information.)

It helps to be as orderly as possible, especially if your cast-plus-crew is more than just yourself, since gear and cases and personal possessions can spread out all over the place very quickly. Assuming you have a "set" where you are filming, here are some things to consider ahead of time:

- What will you do with the memory cards when you are done, or once they are full? (If the equipment is not your own, you want to make sure to take your cards out before the gear goes back to its owners.)

- How will you make a backup copy of the cards once you are done with them? (Do it while still on the set, if at all possible.)

- If you are in a place with other people around, and you don't have a separate security detail, who will keep an eye on things?

- Where will you put empty cases?

- What will you do with lens caps? (Those are so easy to lose track of in a pocket or bag.)

- What will you do with used-up batteries? (And where will you find fresh ones?)

SETTING UP FOR FILMING

Once you arrive at your location, set up to get ready to film. This includes unpacking everything, extending tripod legs, stowing cases in whatever place you've decided on, and getting the camera, the scene, and the performers ready to go.

Now is the time to use the *Loud Dogs* checklist, setting up the lights, placing the camera the right distance from the scene for the first shot, reviewing the shot angle and balance, etc.; setting up the physical components of the camera, and checking and adjusting all the camera settings appropriately.

Once you are set up, take some test shots before you start the actual session and review the footage to make sure everything is working as it should. In an ideal situation, you would have a laptop along and have left enough time to load the footage onto the laptop so you could review it on a bigger screen before you start to film in earnest. That may not always be possible, but it can really help. If you have to review the footage on your camera's tiny screen, at least get the best view possible (through the viewfinder or in a dark place, even if it's under a jacket).

REVIEWING TAKES

During your filming session, you will probably be rushed for time (it always happens) and may feel you don't have time to review what you have filmed while you're on the set. It's unlikely you will be able to review everything, and probably not on a large screen, but you want to review at least the beginning of all your shots as soon as you've taken them — as well as any crucial moments — to make sure it's all going according to plan. (Did you get proper focus for this take? Is the exposure good? Is everyone lumped together on one side of the frame?) Particularly if you are unfamiliar with any of the equipment, don't leave it to fate to see if you recorded footage you can use.

RECORDING TAKES

Except for live performances and some types of conceptual videos, you should be filming the same scene multiple times. Some of the "takes" will go well, but a lot of them will not—and it may be difficult to know what's good or not until you are sitting in front of your computer, long after the cameras have been put away.

MAKING A MUSIC VIDEO REQUIRES ACTING AND LIP-SYNCHING, AND DOING AS MANY TAKES AS YOU NEED TO GET IT RIGHT, EVEN WHEN YOU'RE TIRED.

—Laser Malena-Webber, Musician, Music Video Director

Make sure you record enough takes while you have the chance; that's one of the challenges of the entire process. You may think, "A 3-minute song—how much could I possibly need?" Probably more than you think, especially if you haven't had much filming experience.

> THE AMOUNT OF FOOTAGE YOU ACTUALLY NEED TO SHOOT IS SO UNEXPECTED. I SHOT FOR FOUR HOURS AND HAD JUST ABOUT FOUR MINUTES AND 30 SECONDS' WORTH OF FOOTAGE. SHOT FOOTAGE AND USABLE FOOTAGE ARE COMPLETELY DIFFERENT.
>
> *—Spencer Malley, Musician*

Going back for another day of shooting the same scenes may be overly expensive, or at least impractical, although sometimes that may be the only acceptable choice.

> I HAVE FOUND IT REALLY IMPORTANT TO BE PROUD OF MY PROJECTS. THERE HAVE BEEN TIMES I RUSHED THROUGH FILMING TO MEET A DEADLINE AND WAS NOT EXTREMELY HAPPY WITH THE FOOTAGE. A FEW TIMES, I TOOK NEW FOOTAGE SO I COULD MAKE THE VIDEOS INTO SOMETHING I WAS REALLY EXCITED ABOUT. IT WAS ALWAYS WORTH IT TO TAKE THIS EXTRA TIME.
>
> *—Savannah Philyaw, Indie-Folk Singer-Songwriter*

The alternative—which many of my students have struggled with—is to "stretch" your existing shots (reusing clips, or using less-than-ideal ones), or to drastically alter your original plan so you can come up with enough footage to cover the entire song.

> IT'S SURPRISING THAT YOU CAN NEVER HAVE TOO MANY SHOTS. I HAVE FOUND THAT, WHEN TRYING TO EITHER TELL A STORY OR JUST CREATE A COHESIVE SEQUENCE OF SHOTS, IT CAN FEEL LIKE YOU'RE GRASPING AT STRAWS IF YOU DIDN'T GET ENOUGH SHOTS.
>
> *—Michael Sean Harris, Jamaican Vocalist, Electronic Musician and Educator*

"Slating" is a common filmmaking practice for keeping track of takes—basically, making sure you have visual and audible information about the take, scene, date, etc., as well as a synchronization sound, at the beginning of every take. That may be overkill for most DIY music videos, but the basic idea is good and will make your editing job easier later on.

At the very least, stand in front of the camera and say the take number, which will be recorded on the camera's audio, so you can refer to it later. (If you can write it on a card to show the camera, even better.) It's a good practice to clap once, in case you need a sound for synchronization later on. You can also briefly comment on the previous take. ("That last one was a keeper." or "Dump the last take—it didn't work at all.") If you have an extra crew member, you can record the takes in a notebook, with a brief description of how they went.

> A HARD THING ABOUT MAKING A MUSIC VIDEO IS REPETITION. SOMETIMES YOU PERFORM THE SAME TAKE AT LEAST 20 TIMES BEFORE GETTING IT RIGHT. I WOULD SUGGEST NOTING DOWN YOUR TAKES FOR A SMOOTHER EDIT LATER ON.
>
> *—Dana Fakhoury, Lebanese Musician and Music Producer*

All those takes can be exhausting, so be prepared for the long haul, including having water and maybe food for the cast and crew. (One tradition when using "volunteer" crews is to at least provide them with snacks.)

MULTI-CAMERA FILMING

Filming a scene with multiple cameras has extra challenges. If the shoot involves multiple takes, slating is even more important so you can synchronize the footage during editing. All the cameras should start filming before the take is announced, so each one will record it, and they should all keep running until the end of the take.

We did a multi-camera shoot in a large recording studio, with different students running each of four or five cameras, including a couple that were roaming the studio, shooting handheld. One of the students thought it would be a good idea to stop filming every time he moved from one part of the studio to another, since he wasn't actively focusing or framing the shot and would just have garbage footage. Unfortunately, that meant he had four or five discontinuous clips for every take, making synchronization in post-production extremely difficult. (A better choice is to keep the camera running for the entire song, as it's always easier to sync long clips than short ones.)

FILMING B-ROLL

"B-roll" refers to shots that are supplemental (alternatives) to the main shots. They may be taken before or after the main action, or by a second camera. For example, for a studio performance video, you might get b-roll shots of the people in the recording booth, the mixer board, close-ups of the performers' hands playing their instruments, the entrance to the studio, and other peripheral details connected with the project.

In the editing process, b-roll is useful to fill in places where you don't have primary footage. Maybe at one point in the main shot, something doesn't look right or someone momentarily loses their place in the song. You might be able to use another take, but those spots could also be covered with b-roll. Even in a live recording, b-roll can smooth over rough spots.

3.0: SPECIAL FILMING TECHNIQUES & TRICKS

Along with the basic filming techniques we covered in the previous section, here are some tips and tricks that can expand your creativity and give your music video a unique look. Don't plan to fit in every effect you can find: Be selective and use those that will help you achieve your goals.

WHAT IS THE THREAD THAT BINDS THE WORK TOGETHER? THE EFFECTS?
TOO MANY EFFECTS CREATE A CHAOTIC AND UNPROFESSIONAL LOOK;
A WELL-SELECTED SET OF EFFECTS CAN BE A GOOD WAY TO CREATE
COHESION THROUGHOUT YOUR WORK.

–Pierce Warnecke, Sound and Video Artist and Educator

In this section, we'll look at green screen or chroma key filming, which lets you easily replace parts of your shots with something else. We'll cover time remapping, when you want to speed things up, slow them down, or otherwise play tricks with our usual sense of time. We'll follow that with stop-motion animation, a technique which allows you to make things and people move in unexpected ways, and finish the section with a collection of little tricks that can fool your eye and make your scene extraordinary.

3.1: USING A GREEN SCREEN (CHROMA KEY)

Making it work and avoiding common pitfalls

Green screen

Chroma keying, also known as using a green (or blue) screen, is a technique for layering the images from two different video clips together. Usually, the image in front includes actors or objects that are surrounded by a solid color, typically either blue or green, that is "keyed out" (made transparent) during editing so other images can be placed behind the front subjects.

CHROMA KEY IN MUSIC VIDEOS

Chroma keying is used widely in certain types of productions. For example, weather and news programs often film in front of a green screen to replace the area behind the newscasters with relevant images. Science fiction and action movies use chroma key to be able to easily combine live actors with computer-generated creatures and environments.

For music videos in particular, chroma key can be used to transport the performers to another place and time (such as an exotic beachfront, packed dance hall, or even outer space) that would be too difficult, expensive, or simply impossible to do in real life. Chroma key also makes possible the use of completely abstract backgrounds, and can allow you to add interesting textures and patterns to any object in the foreground that is colored the same as the key.

BLUE SCREEN OR GREEN SCREEN?

The use of blue or green depends on the scene being shot. The idea is that only one color will be keyed out, so it should be as different as possible from the other colors being filmed. Green is a good standard option, although if there are plants in the scene, blue would be a better choice. When I talk about "green screen," the same applies equally to blue screens.

A standard green or blue color is used in the film industry, because these colors are furthest from skin tones and therefore easiest to key out successfully, but any color close to the standard greens or blues will usually make a good key. For example, if you are unable to purchase a standard studio green screen, a solid-color bedsheet, tablecloth, or other large piece of fabric (or even plastic) close to the right color will usually work, as long as you follow the principles of good chroma keying, described below.

THE KEYS TO A GOOD KEY

A good chroma key is one that can be removed completely, leaving the remaining subjects with clean, clear outlines and without leaving patches of semitransparency or glowing green outlines. To make an effective chroma key video, remember the following points.

The keyed color should be as smooth and uniform as possible. If using a cloth, a flat, ironed, seamless surface will key out much more easily than a wrinkled one. If painting a wall for chroma key, the wall should be as free of blemishes, scratches, bumps, ridges, and other irregularities as possible.

The lighting of the keyed surface should also be as even as you can make it, avoiding "hot spots" (areas that are overly bright), shadows, and other inconsistencies. Remember that cameras are much more sensitive to light variations than your eyes, so use your camera's monitor to make sure you are lighting evenly. You will probably need multiple "soft" lights, meaning the light source is as big as possible to spread the light out evenly. (See the chapter on lighting for more information about softening.)

Also, the subject and the green screen should be lit separately, with the subject far enough away from the screen that they don't cast shadows on the background, since that will make the keying out of the background more difficult.

Remember that whatever key color you use, that color should not appear anywhere else in the scene, or those areas will be keyed out as well and appear very strange. For example, if you want a chroma key scene that includes blue clothing, use green or even magenta or hot pink as your key color, as long as the color isn't present in other parts of the scene (including the actor's skin or makeup). Do some test shots and test edits before you fully commit to a production, just to make sure.

You have the most flexibility when the green screen completely surrounds the subject, as it does on professional movie sets, but this requires a lot more green screen and more lighting than would be available to most DIY producers. Still, there are ways to use smaller green screens effectively:

- As long as the area immediately next to the subject is green, the rest of the scene doesn't need to be, since the background can be removed with editing software using a combination of a key effect and a mask. Keep in mind, though, that if the actor is moving, they could easily move so they are no longer surrounded by green.

- A close-up head shot can have a fairly small green screen behind it that is easy to completely key out. For example, a bright green plastic tablecloth could be used.

- Elements that are framed or outlined within the scene can be green and replaced with another scene in post-production. A television weather report is a good example of this, typically with a large green screen in a frame that is replaced with weather footage. You could frame a completely green image inside a mirror, picture frame, or window – or even book covers, computer screens, or clock faces. In these cases, a piece of bright green poster paper cut to shape is often the easiest to work with.

KEYING OUT THE KEY

The method of getting rid of the green screen, or "keying it out," depends on the particular software you use, but most modern video editors can key out a solid color quite easily. You typically have to apply an effect to your video footage, and the effect will probably have "key" somewhere in its name, although there may be other effects that use the word "key," so you should do some research to find out which will give the best results for chroma keying.

For example, recent versions of Adobe Premiere Pro have at least six editing effects with "key" in the title, but "Ultra Key" is the one you want for chroma key work. Adobe After Effects uses a different label, "Keylight."

In most cases, the key effect will allow you to key out any color you choose, so the first step is to use a color picker, such as an eyedropper tool, to select the color you want to key out.

If your key is not perfectly uniform (and they almost never are) because of shadows, wrinkles, and other imperfections, you should pick a color in your scene that approximates the midpoint between the darkest green and the lightest green in your green screen.

Once you have picked the right color, it should become transparent, and you're ready for the next step in the keying process described below. But since the key is rarely perfect, the transparency won't be perfectly transparent, and you will need to make some adjustments to your key. These adjustments differ by software package, but usually you can experiment and adjust each of the parameters you are offered, either up or down, until you get a key you're happy with. If that doesn't work well enough, find an online tutorial on how to use your particular software for chroma keying.

NEXT STEP: REPLACING THE KEY

The whole point of setting up a chroma key is to easily replace part of the footage, often the background, with something else. If you have successfully keyed out the green screen, you can now add another scene beneath or behind the transparent chroma-keyed scene and it will show up in the areas that have been keyed out. For most software packages, there will be multiple horizontal rows on a timeline that can each hold a video track, and the background footage will need to be in a layer below the keyed footage.

If you are trying to make your chroma key look as natural as possible, the lighting on the subject and the lighting in the new background should be similar. As an obvious example, if you have lit your subject with a strong light on the left (producing strong shadows on the right), but your background scene has the sun on the right (producing strong shadows on the left), the resulting composite will look wrong.

GET CREATIVE!

Chroma key can be great for either making something look real that isn't (such as you standing on the beach instead of in your living room), or for doing bizarre things that can be really cool in a music video. For example, if you have an outdoor scene with a uniformly clear blue sky, you might be able to key out the sky and replace it with something completely abstract. You can also use the color picker in your keying effect to pick some color that appears in your scene, and see how many things are made transparent. You probably wouldn't do that in a regular movie, but music videos can be whatever you can imagine, so play around with chroma key and see what you can create!

GREEN SCREEN AT A GLANCE

Chroma key in music videos

Blue or green screen?

Keys to a good key
- Smooth screen
- Even lighting
- No shadows

Keying out the key
- Pick main color
- Make fine-tuning adjustments

Replacing the key

Get creative

3.2: TIME REMAPPING

Time remapping

Time remapping generally refers to altering the appearance of the passage of time in a video, so the action moves faster or slower than normal, including coming to a complete stop.

SPEEDING UP THE VIDEO

Speeding up the video is more than just seeing action move at a faster pace. It can be done in lots of different ways:

- Speed up the action so you can still follow it, but everything moves faster
- Speed up a slowed-down recording of the song, resulting in audio at normal speed while everything else goes much faster than normal
- Speed up the action so much that you can't follow the normal action, but new actions appear (also known as time lapse)
- Combine time lapse with fixed, regular movements to create a hyperlapse

Speed up the action

Speeding up the action of a video so everything moves faster doesn't require anything unusual in the filming process. During the editing phase, simply apply an effect to speed up your clip, typically either by percentage or duration. That is, if you want the video to go twice as fast, change the percentage speed in editing from 100 percent to 200 percent. Alternatively, you could change the duration of a 10-second clip to be compressed to five seconds, which would have the same result.

Video is a collection of individual frames or photographs, shown so quickly one after the other that they give the illusion of movement. If you filmed something at 24 frames per second and sped it up to be twice as fast, you would just be showing every other frame, but played at the same rate so everything appears to be twice as fast. You don't have to worry about the details—the software takes care of the process for you—but the important thing is that there is no loss of quality and nothing special you have to do during filming.

In a music video, you can speed up the action just a little (10 or 20 percent) to give everything an edgier feel. Or you can speed it up a lot (two to five times, that is, 200 percent to 500 percent) to make movements look more artificial. Even higher speeds will make the action look comical. It all depends on the effect you are trying to achieve. (For an example, see the lighting setup in the green screen video accompanying this book.)

If you want to show the vocalist performing the song at the proper speed, even though all the action is sped up, you'll have to take the next step.

Speed up a slowed-down recording of the song

This technique isn't hard, though it takes a little bit of preparation. The end result is a video of you singing or playing a song at normal speed, while everyone and everything around is clearly moving much faster. It could be an effect that's just right for your song.

Preparation

Basically, you create a slowed-down recording of the song—typically anything down to one-quarter speed (25 percent), using the audio software of your choice. (Video software such as Premiere Pro can also be used—just add the song to a timeline, slow it down as you would a video file, then save it as an mp3 file.)

Normally, slowing the song will also lower the pitch dramatically, but most audio software will let you maintain the same pitch as the original recording. It doesn't really matter for the video, although it might be easier to sing along with the song at the original pitch.

Filming

For the video, film as you normally would, but play the slowed recording of the song and sing along with the song at the slower speed. It's not difficult, but plan to practice before filming.

You can also try to move more slowly to match the slower tempo of the song, or you can just move normally while singing slowly. To emphasize the effect, though, you'll want other people in the shots (dancers are great for this) moving normally, or anything where the speed effect will be emphasized in the final product.

Editing

For the editing, speed up the film to compensate for the slower song during the filming. For example, if you sang along to a song that was slowed to one-quarter speed (25%), then speed up the video four times (400 percent) during editing.

Your singing will now match the normal tempo of the song, so when you replace the video soundtrack with your mastered song recording, your mouth movements will match the words of the song. Everything else will be sped up four times, making it look like you are performing in a frenzied world.

Time lapse: super-fast speed

Time lapse video can make normally slow actions, like billowing clouds, look much more dramatic. You can also show action for things that normally move so slowly we don't notice their movement, such as the sun moving across the sky or flowers blooming from bud to fully open in a few seconds.

There are a couple of ways to do time lapse, and each way has different advantages and disadvantages. You can either film normally for a long time and speed everything up a lot, or you can use special software or hardware to film or photograph frames at a much slower rate.

Film it normally and speed it way up

Filming your subject over an extended period and then speeding it up in editing will give you a time-lapse effect. For example, if you want to show the moon moving across the sky during a one-hour period and show it as a five-second clip, film the moon for an hour, then use software or your own calculations to figure out how much to speed it up.

Let's use Premiere Pro as an example. The software can accelerate a clip up to 10,000 percent (100 times) faster. If you film something for 100 minutes, you can speed it up so the action takes place over one minute. In the case of the one-hour (60 minutes, or 3600 seconds) moon shot, you could speed it up 100 times so it plays back in 36 seconds.

If you want to go further, "nest" the sped-up clip, then apply the speed-up effect (called "speed/duration") again to get the clip down to five seconds. (36/5 = 7.2, so speed it up another 720 percent.) If your software doesn't have something similar to nesting, save or export the sped-up clip, then import it as a fresh clip and apply the speed-up effect again.

The main advantage of this approach is that you don't need extra equipment for the filming. The disadvantage, of course, is that you are filming continuously for a very long time, using up lots of battery and storage space. Depending on your situation, you may not have enough battery life or card memory to do it.

Use time-lapse software or hardware

The other option is to use specialized hardware or software to do your time lapse, along with an external battery or continuous power supply (AC connection). This is the only practical option if you want to film something that lasts many hours or even days or weeks, such as a plant growing or a building being constructed.

With time-lapse software/hardware, you take many photos from a fixed position at regular, specified intervals, such as one photo every minute, then combine the photos together so they play back at normal video speeds (24 to 30 frames per second). This gives you the time lapse effect of something moving incredibly fast. Instead of getting rid of frames you don't need (in the previous example), you take only the frames you need to begin with.

This method has the big advantage of being more efficient with storage space, since you are filming only what you need. You could potentially just use your normal battery, but in most cases, you will want a continuous power source, such as an AC adapter, or at least a huge external battery, to make sure your time lapse doesn't die halfway through your project.

If using your phone, your default video app might have a time-lapse setting; if not, you can get one of the many apps available for doing time lapse. When filming, leave it plugged in to a charger if possible.

If using a larger camera, it might have a time-lapse setting built in, or you can use a special piece of hardware that connects to the camera called an "intervalometer." It triggers your camera to take pictures at definable intervals.

In either case, you'll need to use a little math to ensure the results you want. The software may do some of that; the rest will fall to you.

For example, let's say you want to do a time lapse of the moon moving across the entire night sky over an eight-hour period. (You could also do the sun, but pointing your camera at the sun can damage it, so that's a different topic.) You want to make a time lapse of the event that is ten seconds long. So:

> Filming time: 8 hours = 8 x 60 x 60 or 28,800 seconds.
> Edited time: 10 seconds at 24 frames per second, or 240 frames.

Your camera has to take only 240 pictures, but it needs to do it evenly over an eight-hour period. If your software or hardware doesn't do the math for you (that is, let you put in the filming time and the edited time), you need to figure out how long the camera should wait between frames.

> 28,800 seconds/240 frames = 120 seconds/frame

So, you set your time-lapse software or intervalometer to take one picture every 120 seconds (two minutes), and to do it 240 times. That will give you an eight-hour moon shot that plays back in ten seconds.

Hyperlapse (moving time lapse)

A hyperlapse is just a time-lapse video that includes regular, fixed movements between each shot, so the resulting video includes movement.

If you use the "normal filming" method above, the filming will include regular movement, as smooth as possible, while filming. Filming a long road trip from a car window would be one way to do this.

If taking individual pictures for time lapse, you might also use regular movement, such as from a dolly or a motorized slider (a specialized piece of equipment you can program to move a camera slightly between each frame).

A more DIY approach starts with the camera either handheld or on a tripod; you simply move it a fixed distance between each shot. For example, if you are on a walkway with bricks or uniform paving stones, move a certain number of stones between each shot. After every move, re-frame the picture to try and keep the view as consistent as possible. On unmarked ground, use your foot or a stick to keep track of how far you move. (Exactness usually isn't necessary.)

It's unlikely you'll want to do this for an eight-hour moon shot, but you could do a time lapse of a scene with a picture every 15 seconds, moving between each shot, for 15 minutes. This would produce 60 frames, or two seconds of finished video at 30 frames per second. That isn't much, but a hyperlapse doesn't have to be long to make an impact.

Stretch out your work (also useful with stop-motion animation, covered in another chapter) by editing your finished video at 15 or even 10 frames per second. That will make the motion less smooth, but it creates at least twice as much video, so it's worth considering.

SLOWING DOWN THE VIDEO

When slowing down video (for slow motion or "slo-mo" footage), take normal video and use your editing software to slow it down, the flip side of the speeding up described in the previous section.

Slow-motion video has limitations that are different than those of sped-up video. When you speed up video, you need fewer frames than you started with, so the software just has to get rid of the extra frames. To slow video properly, you need to add frames—frames you didn't shoot to begin with.

You could just show each frame for a longer time, but you would lose the smoothness that comes from showing one frame after another at a speed fast enough to look like continuous motion. It would get "stuttery," which may not be the look you want.

For example, if you film at 24 frames per second for one second, and you want to slow your footage by half, the software could show 12 frames during the first second, and 12 frames during the next. But that's only 12 frames per second, which is too slow to look smooth.

Most video editing software will try to make up the difference, and guess (interpolate) what the in-between frames will be.

Imagine you have a ball rolling across the screen. In frame one, it's on the left of the screen, and in frame two, it's on the right. To show the ball rolling more slowly, the software will have to add frames between the ones that are already there.

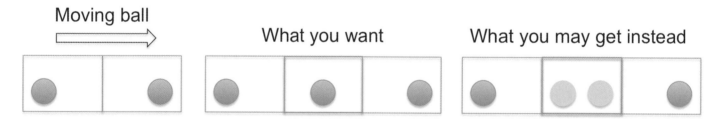

To slow this by half, the software will need to figure out that the extra frame should show the ball in the middle. In this simple example, it might work, but the software might also decide the middle frame should be two balls, one on the left and one on the right, but each one semitransparent. With more complex movement, the job gets much harder, and the results often aren't very satisfactory.

A much better way to do slow motion: Film the original footage at a faster-than-normal rate (frames per second), then play it back at the normal rate. The scene being filmed is happening normally, but the camera records, for example, 60 frames every second rather than 30. When editing the footage, play it back at 30 frames per second so everything is smooth, but plays back at half the speed of the original.

Many cameras film at 120 frames per second (fps) or higher, but typically, the higher the fps, the lower the resolution of the frame. For example, instead of filming in 4K or 1080, the camera might be able to film faster frame rates only at 720, 480, or even less.

The end result is a smooth motion framing at a higher fps, but lower resolution (fewer pixels per square inch), so some sharpness is lost.

As with many technical issues, there are trade-offs, and if your camera doesn't offer the best solution, decide which you prefer: software-created slow motion (same resolution, but possible jerkiness and imperfect "made-up" frames) or frame-rate slow motion with lower resolution.

In a perfect world, or with a really good camera, you can get the higher frame rates at full resolution. You can also rent (or buy, but they are really expensive) very-high-frame-rate cameras that might shoot at thousands of frames per second at full resolution. They can make really cool videos: For example, a three-minute (180-second) music video at 24 fps but filmed at 1200 fps will have all the action happening in just 3.6 seconds. Of course, that will take an insane amount of planning (and dealing with other tricky technical issues) to have 3.6 seconds worth of stuff that would be interesting enough to watch for three minutes, but it has been done successfully (such as OK Go's "The One Moment" video).

Slo-mo variations

Besides slowing down the action a little or a lot, there are a few other possibilities when thinking about slow motion.

- Freeze the action: Take a single frame and hold it. In practice, the software may have an effect that will do this directly, or you may need to take a screenshot of a single frame, and then stretch out that photograph over some period of time. In any case, stop action, then start it up again, which could be effective if there's a dramatic break in the music.

- Slow down (or speed up) the action at variable speeds: This sometimes happens in certain types of action films, and a lot of software will allow something similar in a music video. Because it usually only happens over a second or two—a dramatic slowdown, almost stopping, then speeding up faster than normal before the normal action resumes— it can often be done with footage that has been filmed normally. If you want the footage to look really smooth, film at a higher frame rate as described above.

- Slow down a sped-up recording of a song: This is the reverse of the process described above under "speeding up." It is a bit more of a challenge, since you would want to film at a higher frame rate (which may need a special camera) and also sing or play a song at a higher speed, which can be a lot harder than slowing down. In the playback, it would look like you were singing normally while everyone around you is moving in slow motion, so it's fun if you can do it.

TIME REMAPPING AT A GLANCE

Speeding up

- Speed up the action
- Speed up a slowed-down recording
- Time lapse
- Hyperlapse

Slowing down

- Film at higher frame rate
- Variations
  - Freeze frame
  - Variable speed
  - Slow down a sped-up recording

3.3: STOP-MOTION ANIMATION

Getting anything to move

Stop motion

WHAT EXACTLY IS STOP-MOTION ANIMATION?

Stop-motion animation makes things move in ways you don't expect. It involves moving an object or person in small increments and filming the non-moving state after each movement, then combining each shot in post-production to create animated movement.

The traditional method for stop-motion animation is to take a photograph after each movement, and combine the photos in post. For the smoothest possible stop motion, the camera should be triggered remotely so it is not jiggled each time the shutter is released.

An easier method for recording stop motion, and usually easier for a DIYer to do successfully, is to take a continuous video and remove what you don't want in the editing phase. This is explained in detail below.

BIG ANIMATION VS. SMALL ANIMATION

One way to think of stop-motion animation is big vs. small.

- Big stop-motion animation generally involves people moving in ways that look strange or magical, such as sliding along the ground without moving their feet, or even floating through the air. The movements are combined in such a way that they look both natural and unnatural at the same time.
- Small stop motion involves small objects or miniatures of larger objects that are manipulated by hand, one small move at time, so that when they are animated, it looks like they are moving on their own.

When we talk about stop-motion animation below, assume we're talking about small animation—some small inanimate object made to look as though it is moving under its own power. In the filming stage, those objects are moved with your hands.

STOP-MOTION ANIMATION USING VIDEO

While traditional stop-motion animation uses individual photographs stitched together in post-production, this method requires that each picture be taken without unplanned movement of the camera. (There may be situations when jerky animation is wanted, so moving the camera each time wouldn't be a problem.) If there's no remote control for the camera and you have to physically push the shutter button each time, keeping the camera still is nearly impossible. Here are two alternate methods that will overcome that problem.

Alternate #1: "Twin blade" stop motion

"Twin blade," the first alternate method, is easiest to film with no special equipment, although the editing is more tedious. Basically, continuously film the entire stop-motion process, then cut out everything but the exact frames you want (with a cut on each side of those frames, which is why I call it "twin blade").

Set the camera on a tripod, pointing toward the action you will create, then let the camera run as the objects or people move or are moved at your own pace. Each time there is a move, be sure that anyone or anything extra gets completely out of the camera frame (including shadows!) so there is at least one clean frame that can be isolated to use for the animation. The frame selected in editing will be equivalent to what would have been photographed using the traditional method.

The time-consuming part comes in the editing, when each good frame on the timeline is located and cut on each side of it. Once you have cut out each frame, select all the footage between those cuts (for example, in Premiere Pro, using command + click for each section of footage), then do a ripple delete to get rid of all the unwanted footage and simultaneously close the gaps between the frames.

It takes time, but with that step the basic editing is done, and you will have a stop-motion video. From there, adjust the speed (see below) or apply any other editing and effects.

Alternate #2: "Metronome" stop motion

If you are careful with your motions and can make each move precisely according to a fixed beat, you can greatly simplify the editing process, although the filming has to be better planned. With this method, play a metronome to make sure each move matches a beat, so in post processing, you just have to find the right starting point and speed up the video according to some simple calculations.

For the sake of keeping the explanation simple, we'll assume you are filming at 30 frames per second (fps). The method works for any frame rate, but the math isn't as even.

Assume you can move your object (and get out of the frame), or have the actors move, once every couple of seconds, so you could move the object 30 times per minute. Think of it as filming at 30 frames per minute rather than 30 frames per second, or 1/60 the normal film speed.

To make the object moves in strict time, set up a metronome (such as a free metronome app on your phone) and move on the beat. Having a 4/4 measure (so 30 x 4, or 120 beats per minute, with a stronger sound on beat 1), moving once per measure, is a good way to make sure your moves are even.

- On beat 1, you do the movement, whatever it is (a person or object)
- On 2, you get anything extra out of the frame
- On 3, you pause (this will be the frame that the stop motion uses)
- On 4, you prepare to make the next move

It can be helpful to actually count out loud with the metronome so you don't get mixed up—"one and hold and" on 1, 2, 3, 4, respectively— since the action moves along steadily and it's easy to get confused. With each new measure, increase the count by one ("two and hold and, three and hold and…") so you can keep track of how many frames there will be in the end.

A note about planning time

At a finished rate of 30 fps, move an object 30 times for one second of action. You can often get away with a slower effective frame rate—15 or even 10 frames per minute, as explained below—but it will be jerkier, and 30 fps is a good goal.

So, if you want a finished clip with five seconds of footage, that will be 30 moves x 5 or 150 moves. You will make 30 moves each minute, so that is five minutes of filming, making a move every two seconds and counting up to 150.

If you've managed to make the moves successfully, 30 times per minute on a strict beat (and getting out of the frame each time), then the editing is a matter of identifying the right beginning frame (the first "hold" count) and then speeding up the video by 6,000 percent (or 60 x 100%).

That may sound like a lot, but Premiere Pro (and probably most other editing software) can speed up footage up to 10,000 percent with a couple of clicks, and it's nearly instantaneous. Once the clip is sped up, play it back to make sure you didn't accidently get unwanted movement in one of the frames; then the basic editing is done. If it doesn't quite work, adjust the starting frame by a few frames, then try again.

ADJUSTING THE SPEED OF STOP-MOTION VIDEO

Once the stop-motion clips are in an animated sequence, you may find the action moves too quickly. Especially if an object is being moved by hand, it's hard to anticipate how small the movement needs to be in order to get natural-looking movement over a period of time.

The best way to fix that may be to film the sequence again, since beginning animation involves a lot of trial and error. But if you just want to slow down what you have, here are the steps:

1. If you sped up the footage (to 6000 percent), you can't just slow it down, because there will be unwanted movement in the frames.

2. Instead, regardless of how the stop motion was edited, select all the relevant clips on the timeline and nest the footage, which groups all the individual clips into one clip.

3. On the master timeline, now change the speed. Slowing the footage to 50 percent will give 15 fps if you started with 30. Slowing to 33 percent will give 10 fps. The footage will look more jerky, but it often looks fine, although more obviously like stop motion and less like smooth animation.

STOP MOTION AT A GLANCE

Big vs. small animation

Stop motion using video

- "Twin blade" stop motion
- "Metronome" stop motion
- Adjusting the speed

3.4: MORE SPECIAL EFFECTS

Light painting & bokeh, Forced perspective, 90-degree gravity shift

Special effects (SFX), also called practical or in-camera effects, are created during filming using special techniques to create something not possible — or at least not expected — from normal live action. (The term visual effects, or VFX, typically refers to effects created completely in post-processing.) Although SFX are created "in-camera," most of them require editing work in post-production as well. For specifics about achieving any of these effects you can find detailed instructions online. This summary gives an idea of a few of the techniques that are possible.

BOKEH

Bokeh comes from the Japanese term for blur or haze, and refers to the blur of an image that is out of focus. The blur is especially pronounced on small bright lights against a dark background, and is commonly used in night shots with traffic lights or Christmas lights, producing blurred discs of light.

If you want an entire image of bokeh, un-focus the lens completely. If you want a sharp image against a background of bokeh lights, you'll want a lens with a low f-stop (such as 2.8 or lower) that can produce a shallow depth of field. Different lenses produce different shapes, usually approximations of a circle, depending on the internal construction of the lens and how close the highlights are to the center of the lens.

You can make special "shaped bokeh" by creating filters in different shapes for your lens. It's a little complicated, but there are some good tutorials online (search for "shaped bokeh"). You can see what is possible using this technique by watching Gramatik's "Solidified" music video.

FOG OR SMOKE

Fog machines are inexpensive to rent or buy and can add great atmosphere to a video. Dry ice (frozen carbon dioxide) in water can also create an attractive mist that stays near to the ground. If filming outdoors, particularly in a rural area, an orchard fogger could be an option if you can find one to rent or borrow.

For any foggy or smoky shot, the lighting will make a big difference. You will get the most dramatic results by shooting at night with portable lights that you can move around to see which angle works best. Bright lights shining from one side can create a great effect, as well as light behind the subject shining directly towards the camera through the mist.

FORCED PERSPECTIVE

Forced perspective lets you alter the apparent sizes of people or things being filmed. Using a high f-stop for a deep depth-of-field (objects both close and far away are in focus) and careful positioning, things closer to the camera will appear larger, and those farther away will appear smaller, but both near and far objects will appear to be in the same plane. This technique can be used to make dwarfs or giants out of regular people and monsters out of toys.

A common example of forced perspective is when a tourist stands next to the leaning tower of Pisa, looking like they are nearly as tall as the tower and holding it up with their hand. In *The Lord of the Rings* movies, forced perspective was used to make Frodo look much smaller than Gandalf, even though in real life the height difference between the actors is a matter of five inches.

LENS FLARES

Lens flares occur when a bright light shines directly or nearly directly into a lens, producing light aberrations on the image that appear as colored streaks, lines, and circles.

Traditionally, lens flares were a mistake to be avoided, but they are used on purpose in many film and video productions for a dramatic effect. They can also be added as effects in post-processing, although real, in-camera lens flares have a unique appearance.

To produce them on purpose, the sun or another bright light source should be shining close to or directly into the lens as you film. In addition to positioning the camera, try using a flashlight or other handheld light to create lens flares.

LIGHT PAINTING

Light painting is more of a photographic technique, but it can be applied to video as well. Light painting refers to taking a long-exposure photograph while either moving a light source in front of the camera, or moving the camera while pointed at a light source. The resulting photograph shows the entire path of the moving light source during the time of the exposure.

Silhouette created from a 10-second-long exposure of moving fairy lights

Light painting is typically done at twilight, sunrise, during the night, or in a dark space. To paint with light, either have the camera on a tripod, if painting with a moving light source, or hold the camera by hand, if using fixed light sources.

In either case, the camera should be pre-focused so the source of the light is in focus (unless you want to do light painting with a bokeh effect). The camera is set to fully manual exposure, with a long-enough exposure to produce the desired effect. This may be as short as one second, or as long as you need. Expose the image long enough (with the right aperture or f-stop) so you only see the light trail against a black background, or expose it long enough to see the surrounding landscape as well. Experiment with a few test shots, using different combinations of aperture and shutter speed, to see what works best.

For moving light sources, use small flashlights, either alone or shining into larger translucent (plastic) containers, with or without color filters. If moving the camera, then any scene with multiple sources of light against a darker background, such as street lights, can work well.

There are a couple of ways to apply light painting to a video. Particularly if there are light streaks against a dark background, overlay the images of light streaks onto other images for one or more frames of the video. (For example, in Premiere Pro, this would be done by changing the Opacity blend mode from Normal to Lighten or something similar.)

Alternatively, take multiple frames of a light painting with the intention of combining them together in post-production as stop-motion animation. This can create an impressive effect, although since each frame takes at least a few seconds, plus the time between frames, getting enough frames for a 24-frame-per-second animation can take quite a long time.

PROJECTION MAPPING

Using a digital projector, you can project images onto instruments, performers, or the entire set, providing another layer of images for your video. Any video or photo can be projected to create fascinating effects on your set.

The music video "Style" by Taylor Swift uses this effect (along with mist and smoke) to produce some very cool images.

WET PLATE OR WET TANK EFFECTS

These effects use ink or paint to create organic, swirling shapes and colors in water.

For wet plate effects, a sheet of clear glass is laid flat with space underneath it, with a camera positioned directly above it, pointing down. The area underneath is covered with a black cloth, and a light source is positioned to the side, either underneath or above, depending on the desired look.

A thin film of water is spread on the glass, then ink, paint, food coloring, and other colored liquids are added to the water (using a dropper, spoon, etc.) while the glass is being filmed. Different effects and animations can be achieved using different substances, including dishwashing detergent, oil, and milk.

For a wet tank effect, a clear glass tank (such as a fish tank or large clear bottle) is filled with water, and various liquids are dropped into it while it is filmed from the side. Strong side lighting is useful for bringing out the most contrast.

The wet tank effect can be much more dramatic than the wet plate effect, although it is much easier to clean off a wet sheet of glass to try something different than it is to empty a tank of water, clean it, and fill it again for another experiment.

360-DEGREE VIDEO

360-degree video, where you can virtually "spin around" to watch different parts of a video as if you were in the center of a complete circle, is a unique way of presenting a music video. Many online platforms support 360 video, where you can circle around in the video using a mouse in a regular browser window, or, with a virtual reality (VR) headset, just by looking in different directions.

A 360 video usually requires a special camera as well as a lot of special post-processing. However, you can use a regular camera (more below), and the processing is getting easier.

There are two main artistic considerations with a 360 video:

1. The principles of scene composition are different, since you aren't dealing with a fixed rectangle, and you don't really know where the viewer will be looking at any given time.

2. To make a 360 video worth the trouble, you should have interesting and unique views regardless of which direction the viewer is looking. If all of the main action is in one part of the 360-degree view, there is no reason to look anywhere else.

One attraction of 360 video is that viewers can choose their own experience. But we're not used to telling stories or creating art (at least linear art, like a music video) in that way, and it's a challenge to create something the audience will really enjoy and view multiple times to see what is available on all sides.

When planning a 360 video, think about what would make sense and be interesting regardless of which way you looked. Try giving each member of the band their own section of the 360-degree scene, or have the band on one side, dancers on another, and other related or random things spaced around the circle.

Filming in 360 degrees

Filming a 360 video is easiest with a specialty 360 camera, but 360 cameras that also create high-quality images are quite expensive and may be hard to find, even as a rental. As an alternative, use a regular camera to film four different scenes meant to be played simultaneously, then stitch them together as if they were four sides of a square room, with the viewer in the center. You can also film scenes for the ceiling and the floor of your virtual room.

Whether there's 360 footage or multiple two-dimensional clips you want to join together, post-processing is necessary, unless the camera does it automatically. Versions of Adobe After Effects from 2018 on have built-in functionality to let you process your videos for YouTube or other platforms that allow 360 video.

90-DEGREE GRAVITY SHIFT

The idea of this effect is that the camera is turned 90 degrees from its normal position—either on its side, or pointing straight down—to record action that appears to defy the laws of gravity.

A specially built set can make these effects look more real, but even when the setup is more lo-fi and obviously fake, it can still be interesting.

Overhead shift

The overhead shift requires that a camera be rigged fairly high above a plain surface, like a solid-color floor or a tarp. The camera rigging, which must be some distance directly above the performers, is the most difficult part, but once that is in place, the actors can lie on the ground, moving as if they were standing up but in unusual ways. This setup is usually combined with stop-motion animation to create even more creative results. Oren Lavie's music video, "Her Morning Elegance," is a great example of what can be done with this technique. (Also see the 90-degree gravity shift video for this book.)

Sideways shift

For the sideways effect, one approach is to have a ground surface that looks something like a wall, with a plain background that doesn't indicate a specific orientation. With the camera on its side, it will look like you are walking or crawling up a wall.

Also, if there's a wall intersecting the ground or floor, the actors can sit, lean, or move around against the wall (which is actually the ground) for more interesting effects.

MORE SPECIAL EFFECTS AT A GLANCE

Bokeh

Fog or smoke

Forced perspective

Lens flares

Light painting

Projection mapping

Wet plate/tank effects

360-degree video

90-degree gravity shift
- Overhead
- Sideways

4.0: POST-PRODUCTION

Finishing your video

Video post-production involves everything that happens after the camera is put away. This includes editing, of course, but also media management, adding titles and graphics, creating post-production special effects, and color correction and grading.

AS MUCH WORK AS SHOOTING A MUSIC VIDEO CAN BE, WITH SCHEDULING, LOCATION SCOUTING, SETUP, LIGHTING, AND ALL OF THE LOGISTICAL AND ARTISTIC FACTORS, THAT'S REALLY THE EASY PART. POST-PRODUCTION IS EVERY BIT AS IMPORTANT, AND CAN BE JUST AS DIFFICULT IN ITS OWN WAY, AND EVEN MORE TIME-CONSUMING. THE POSSIBILITIES ARE ENDLESS, AND MANY OF THEM WON'T EVEN OCCUR TO YOU UNTIL YOU SEE THE FIRST AND SECOND CUT.

—Stephen Webber, Executive Director, BerkleeNYC

Post-production involves six major steps:

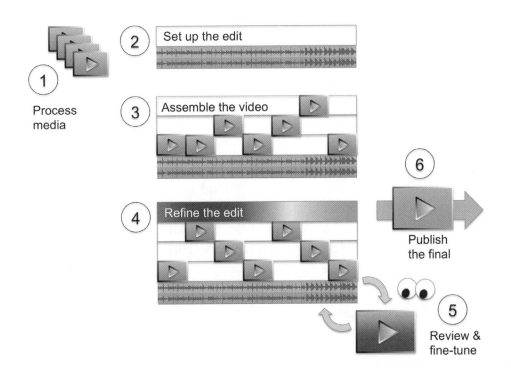

Post-production can be a daunting process, but grouping it into major steps can help make it more manageable.

1. Process the media files, ranking and renaming the good ones and getting rid of the bad ones.

2. Set up the edit in the software of your choice. This includes importing media, creating a timeline, and processing the main song file for the video.

3. Assemble the video from the building blocks of your media files. This step can also include adding effects, transitions, and color correcting. This requires the most time, and it is where the magic starts to happen.

4. Refine the edit, making the video that much better by tweaking cuts and transitions, doing color grading, and adding titles and credits.

5. Export the video, review it (alone and with others), then return to editing to fine-tune it further.

6. After one or more sessions of review and refinement, export the final video.

For the DIY producer, we'll also include "distribution and promotion" in this section. That may just mean uploading the video to your YouTube channel and Facebook page, although there are other steps that will help the world see what you have created. We'll go over the basics and key success factors.

4.1 POST-PRODUCTION STEPS

MEDIA MANAGEMENT AND PROCESSING

For a large, complicated production, good media management is crucial, since there are hundreds of files that need to be accounted for. For your video project, there probably won't be hundreds of files, but there could easily be dozens. If your creation involves multiple scenes and many takes of each scene, the files add up quickly. Even if there are only a few files, taking the time to review and process them now will save steps later.

Copy and backup

Ideally, the files were copied and backed up during the shoot, but if not, now is the time to do it. Make sure you at least have your working files on the computer you will be using or on an external drive, and a backup copy on another device or online (although you will want a very fast connection, because the files are huge). Making backups is never very interesting, but if there's only one copy of the files and you lose them or they become corrupted, the Production phase has to be done all over again. (Ask my students about how fun that is.)

Review and rename

Once you have your copies and backups, go through all the media files to see what's there. This can use the simplest video player available on your computer. The goals are: 1) to delete any files that are clearly unusable; 2) to rank and rename the remaining files.

Name the files by the scene or some other descriptor that is meaningful and consistent, as well as by the take number. I also like to rank or score the files: A for shots that look great and that I'll definitely want to use, B for shots that have some potential, and sometimes C for shots that I don't want to delete even though they're marginal at best. An example might be "A beach party 01.mov," so all the A files will be grouped together in an alphabetical list. If there are lots of media files, you may want to sort them into folders on your storage device to make them easier to access later.

> PERSONALLY, I TEND TO GET STARTED WITHOUT A SET PLAN, SO THE EDITING SESSION CAN GET VERY MESSY. IT WOULD SAVE ME A LOT OF TIME IF I NAMED ALL FILES PROPERLY, WATCHED THEM THROUGH, AND PREPARED THE VIDEO IN DETAIL (NOT ONLY IN MY HEAD) BEFORE GETTING STARTED.
>
> *—Eli Gauden, Norwegian Singer-Songwriter*

Collect other media files

Besides the files from your cameras, in most cases there will be a master song file that will form the bedrock of the video. There may also be photographs, archive or stock footage, or other media. Gather them at the beginning (and make backups), so you don't have to track them down later.

SETTING UP THE EDIT

Choose software

The editing software used depends on a number of factors, including what is available, accessible, and what you have experience with. If you are a student, your school may have editing software available on school computers. Software might also be available at your local library or other common space. (Our local library has a makerspace with the latest version of the Adobe suite, for instance.)

For professional-level editing, the most popular options are Adobe Premiere Pro, Apple Final Cut (Macintosh only), and Avid Media Composer. On the other extreme, free options include iMovie (on a Mac), HitFilm Express, and free versions of Avid and DaVinci Resolve. Midrange consumer packages include Pinnacle Studio and Corel VideoStudio, along with many others. Free software is often inadequate for what you have in mind, but it can be an easy place to start if you have no experience with any software package.

Open and import

Whatever software you are using, the first steps are to open the program and import the media files. If you have sorted them into folders, you may be able to import entire folders so you can keep the same organization within your editing program. I also like to set up separate folders (called "bins" in Premiere Pro) for any files that might be better grouped together, like photos, audio files, etc. During the editing process, I also create new bins for grouping whenever I see that I have more than two or three items of the same type in the project window.

Create the timeline

Creating the main timeline is the next logical step in the editing process. How it is created depends on the software used, but you want to have the same movie size (resolution and frame rate) as the footage you filmed. Most software will adjust for different movies sizes on the same timeline, but consistency increases the chances of getting the best possible output.

If there are different clips at different sizes, decide which to use for your main timeline. Generally, you should create a timeline with high definition (1080 minimum), even if you have a number of historical clips that are only standard definition.

Prepare the main song file

In most cases, the song file that you plan to use will have been mixed and mastered separately, so you just have to place the file on the timeline. If there are performance clips that need to be synchronized exactly with the audio file, some programs will do the synchronization automatically, so you may do that before or in place of adding the audio file directly to the timeline.

If clips have to be synchronized manually, add a clip with its audio file to the timeline, along with the main audio file, and use both audible cues (listening to both audio files at once) and visual cues (looking at the waveform of each audio file, if available) to line them up.

ASSEMBLING THE VIDEO

I'VE BEEN SURPRISED AT HOW FUN EDITING CAN BE. THE RIGHT EDITS CAN MAKE A HUGE DIFFERENCE IN THE OVERALL PIECE. AS SOMEONE MORE ACCUSTOMED TO BEING ON THE LIVE PERFORMANCE SIDE OF THINGS, I WAS SURPRISED TO FIND THAT EDITING IS REALLY ENJOYABLE FOR ME.

–Shaudi Bianca Vahdat, American/Iranian Musician and Theatre Artist

Add media files to the timeline

Selecting and adding clips to your timeline, and deciding where to cut from one clip or scene to the next, is the basic job of the editor. It's where you use your creativity and bring to life your artistic vision, like putting together a puzzle where you get to decide where each piece goes to make the picture you want. Because it is so fundamental, any software package should make this part of the editing job fairly simple.

There are different ways of adding clips to a timeline, but here are some of the most basic.

1. Dragging or placing an entire clip on the timeline, then trimming, cutting, and adjusting the clip on the timeline.

2. Selecting a portion of a clip (a beginning and ending point) in a preview or source window, then manually placing that clip on the timeline.

3. Selecting a portion of a clip and inserting it wherever the timeline marker or playhead is on the timeline. (An insertion will "push" any clips after it further along the timeline, so nothing is replaced, but everything that is beyond the playhead position is shifted later to make space for the new clip. Think of it like a person cutting into a line.)

4. As above, but overwriting rather than inserting, so any clip on the timeline where the new clip goes will be replaced by the new clip. (Like someone getting into a line by pulling someone out and taking their place, so no one else in the line has to shift places.)

I THINK THE MOST IMPORTANT THING ABOUT MAKING A MUSIC VIDEO IS TRYING TO MATCH MUSICAL PHRASES – EMOTIONAL MOMENTS IN THE MUSIC, PAUSES AND HIGH POINTS – WITH THE VISUALS. I FIND IT TO MAKE A BIG DIFFERENCE WHEN THESE THINGS LINE UP.

–Eli Gauden, Norwegian Singer-Songwriter

Add transitions

The "cut" is the most basic type of transition, where one video clip stops on one frame and another clip starts on the next frame. In slower, more moody pieces of music, a "dissolve" transition is sometimes used, where the footage changes gradually from one scene to the next over a few frames. There are also other types of scene transitions, and your software package may have dozens of them available (wipes, slats, zig-zags, swirls, and more), but for the most part, a simple cut is the preferred (and more professional) way to change from one scene to the next.

Where and when to cut

Cut timing can range from one cut every frame (resulting in a strobe-like effect that works only for certain types of music) to no cuts during the entire video (a "single-shot" music video, where the entire video is a single take from one camera). A single-shot video may sound attractive because it is easy to edit, but it needs careful planning and flawless execution in the production phase, usually requiring a lot of takes to get it right.

Most editing falls somewhere between those two extremes, with a given scene lasting anywhere from less than a second to a few seconds. Watch other videos of a similar genre, and keep track of how often they cut between scenes and the duration of a typical scene; that's a good way to gain experience in cutting a video. (Beginner videos tend to have longer clips than professional ones.)

Cuts typically come on the beat or at the start or end of musical phrases. Cuts can also be dictated by the action on the screen (as in regular film), but the music rather than the action usually drives the cuts.

MAKE SURE THE VISUAL HIGHLIGHTS THE RIGHT FOCUS ON THE RIGHT MOMENT AND FLOW WITH THE DYNAMIC OF THE MUSIC, SUCH AS SHOWING THE SOLOIST AND THE REACTION OF THE ACCOMPANIST, AND CUT WITH THEIR MUSICAL PHRASE. USE FAST CUTS FOR HIGH ENERGY MOMENTS.

–Simon Yu, Musician, Music Video Director

Make it a priority to choose places for cuts that seem natural and don't call attention to themselves (unless that is the goal). Once all of the basic cuts are in place, it's helpful to have someone other than the editor review them to see if the cuts seem to match the music and if the scenes change frequently enough to keep the video interesting.

REFINING THE EDIT

I HAVE FOUND IT REALLY HELPFUL TO SPEND LOTS OF TIME EDITING. EDITING TOOK THE MAJORITY OF MY TIME. I PLAYED AROUND WITH SO MANY DIFFERENT OPTIONS FOR TRANSITIONS, SEQUENCES OF SCENES, AND EFFECTS. IT WAS AMAZING TO SEE HOW EACH OF THESE LITTLE DIFFERENCES HAD SUCH DIFFERENT EMOTIONAL EFFECTS ON THE VIDEO. IT'S LIKE WRITING AND EDITING A SONG. THERE ARE SO MANY POSSIBILITIES AND A SIMPLE CHANGE OF A CHORD, LYRIC, OR MELODY, CAN TURN AN AVERAGE SONG INTO A HIT.

—Savannah Philyaw, Indie-Folk Singer-Songwriter

Add effects

Visual effects (or VFX) are similar to special effects (SFX), but are primarily added in the post-production stage. For example, using a green screen is considered VFX, since the screen is replaced digitally in post-production, even though it requires a special setup during filming as well.

Editing programs generally have some limited VFX available, such as basic green screen removal and replacement, as well as artificial lighting effects like lens flares and lightning.

More dramatic results require specialized programs such as Adobe After Effects and Apple Motion. Even more complicated 3D modeling and animation, also known as CGI (computer-generated imagery), is possible using programs such as Cinema 4D, Maya, and Blender.

These programs have amazing capabilities, and so they each require a considerable investment in time and money (except for Blender, which is freeware) to learn them. If you are willing to put in the time, there are online tutorials for just about anything you might want to do.

Tweak the cuts and transitions

After making the initial placement of video clips, go back and see how they can be refined and improved. If you are trying to cut right on the beat or exactly where a big moment happens in the music, and find that it's slightly off, play with it a little. You may decide two clips need to be swapped, or one section just isn't working, and you want to go back and review other footage to find something that works better.

Do color correction and color grading

Color correction usually takes place after the editing and other effects are done. Color correction attempts to get the color of your video as close to "real life," or what you actually saw when you filmed, as possible. Getting accurate skin tones is one of the chief goals of color correction.

After color correction is complete, color grading can be added to give the overall video a specific look and mood. Color grading can really add polish to the video and make it look unique and professional.

In both steps, you may adjust exposure, color, saturation, hue, contrast, and white balance. Work on all of the values overall, or focus on values in a specific range, including highlights, mid-tones, shadows, whites, or blacks. Since every change is reversible, play around (and take tutorials) to gain experience with what is possible. If you can use a monitor calibrated to show accurate color, that will be a big advantage in this process.

Add titles and credits

During the first five seconds or so of a video, include a title that gives the name of the artist and the song. This can be just the title itself, on a plain background before the video starts, or overlaid in the lower third of the screen as the video begins. Including the title and the artist's name is free advertising, reinforcing the artist's identity. All modern video editing software should include a way to easily add text and simple graphics to your screen.

For the end credits, consider listing the name of the director and any other people involved in the creation of the video. This is optional, but it is a nice way to acknowledge those who have helped.

REVIEWING AND FINE-TUNING

THE BIGGEST THING I LEARNED FROM MAKING/BEING IN A MUSIC VIDEO IS THAT SOMETIMES DONE IS BETTER THAN PERFECT. I HAVE WASTED COUNTLESS HOURS TRYING TO MAKE MY VIDEO LOOK ABSOLUTELY PERFECT TO ME THAT WON'T NECESSARILY MATTER TO THE VIEWER. TEST THE VIDEO ON SOMEONE YOU TRUST TO GIVE YOU AN HONEST OPINION. YOU'LL FIND THAT ALL THE NITTY-GRITTY STUFF THAT BOTHERS YOU DOESN'T EVEN GET NOTICED BY THEM. YES, THE VIDEO SHOULD LOOK GOOD, BUT JUST MAKE SURE YOU'RE NOT WASTING YOUR TIME ON SOMETHING THAT DOESN'T MATTER.

—Steve Umculo, South African Musician and Entertainer

After you're satisfied with the video, at least for the short term (or sometimes, when you're tired of working any more on it), it's a good time to export it and show it to others for their review. If you're making the music video for someone else, this is the point to show them what you have created (unless they've been helping you all along with the process). Definitely show it to anyone who has a stake in the outcome, but also try to find some fresh eyes to look at the video—someone unfamiliar with what you've been doing. They may be able to provide a valuable perspective.

Since it's impossible to please everyone, and it wouldn't be useful to try, distinguish between those who have a final say and those who just have opinions. Even so, if your goal is the broadest appeal possible, the comments of a random friend or two could be very valuable.

In nearly every case, plan to go back to the editing table and do another round of fine-tuning, based on the feedback received. Whether you do it a second or third time depends on you and your circumstances, but strive to get to a point where all the important parties are happy with the results.

PUBLISHING THE FINAL VIDEO

The final steps of the production process are to export your footage, and then archive your footage so you have a backup copy of anything that is relevant. This would generally include all of the raw video clips, sound files, and other media that you used in the video, as well as the files saved by the editing program.

When you export, there are a few decisions that you need to make:

- Movie size
- Format
- Bitrate

Movie size

You chose a movie size, including resolution (such as 1080p or 4K) and frame rate (probably 24, 25, or 30 frames per second) for filming as well as for editing. In most cases, you will have chosen the same settings for each stage, and keep those settings for the final export. This will preserve the best possible quality of the finished product.

There may be some situations where the exported movie size needs to be changed. For instance, you might need a file small enough to send via email, or for a specialized device; in such a case, decrease the resolution, for example, from 1920 x 1080 to 960 x 540 (one-quarter the resolution, which would be one-quarter the file size). This will cause a much lower quality, of course, so resort to this only if you have a good reason to do so.

If you want your 1080 video to look good on a 4K screen, it might be tempting to increase the resolution when exporting. This is rarely a good idea—unless you use specialized software for that purpose, it won't look any better and will just make a much larger file.

Format

When exporting a file, choose a format, which consists of a container and a codec. The container is the type of file that "contains" the video and is usually indicated by the file name extension, such as .mp4, .mov, or .avi. The "codec" (which comes from "coder/decoder") is the method used to store the file electronically, usually by compressing it so it doesn't take up so much disk space, then decompressing the file so you can watch it.

A current popular format for exporting videos to be shown online is the H.264 codec within an .mp4 container (which is what YouTube and Vimeo recommend). If you are creating a music video for broadcast or some other platform, they may have a different preferred format, so it is best to find out what the final platform requires.

To make a high-quality archival copy of your footage, choose a "lossless" format, which means no information is lost during the coding/decoding process. (H.264 is a "lossy" format, meaning some information is discarded during the file conversion, although it is still a fairly high-quality format.) The lossless formats available depend on the program used; they will create files much larger than other formats, but are a good choice if there's a chance you will need to use your video in a different format in the future.

Bitrate

The bitrate basically describes the rate of information flow (bits per second) for displaying the video. Higher bitrates mean higher quality but also larger files (and potentially slower downloads and streaming). If there is more information, such as higher resolution (more pixels on the screen) or a higher frame rate (more pixels every second), higher bitrates are required.

In practical terms, different websites give recommendations for the preferred bitrate for videos to be uploaded, so search for "recommended bitrate for [website of choice]." For example, YouTube lists 8 Mbps for 1080p videos at up to 30 fps, 12 Mbps for 1080p at 48-60 fps, 35-45 Mbps for 4K videos at up to 30 fps, etc.

These are recommended minimums. You may find that, after the video is exported and uploaded, the quality isn't as good as you had hoped; in this case, re-export the video with a higher bitrate setting. The exporting function in the editing software should allow the option of changing the bitrate when you set up your video export.

POST-PRODUCTION STEPS AT A GLANCE

Media management and processing

- Copy and backup
- Review and rename
- Collect other media files

Setting up the edit

- Choose software
- Open and import
- Create the timeline
- Prepare the main song file

Assembling the video

- Add media files to the timeline
- Add transitions
- Where and when to cut

Refining the edit

- Add effects
- Tweak the cuts and transitions
- Do color correction and grading
- Add titles and credits

Reviewing and fine-tuning

Publishing the final video

- Movie size
- Format
- Bitrate

4.2: DISTRIBUTION AND PROMOTION

THE BEST PART ABOUT MAKING A MUSIC VIDEO IS WHEN IT'S DONE! THE END PRODUCT AND THE RELEASE IS THE MOST EXCITING PART, PROVIDED ITS GOOD!

—Oliver Kersey, British Singer-Songwriter

Music videos have always been about promoting the music and the artist who makes it, primarily through building a fanbase that includes people willing to pay for recordings and come to performances.

Your video can't begin doing the job of promoting your music until it's distributed, so it's important to spread the word. Social media sites are the principal vehicles to distribute a music video, although there are other ways—discussed below—to use your music video.

POSTING CONSISTENTLY ON YOUTUBE AND FOLLOWING THROUGH WITH PROMOTION IS IMPORTANT TO GETTING VIEWS; YOU CAN'T JUST POST SOMETHING AND RUN AWAY. EVEN A BAD MUSIC VIDEO WITH A GOOD MARKETING PLAN IS GOING TO DO MORE FOR YOU THAN SOMETHING INCREDIBLE THAT NOBODY KNOWS ABOUT.

—Laser Malena-Webber, Musician, Music Video Director

The social media landscape is continually shifting. YouTube remains the primary outlet for showing music videos, but other sites can also be important, so we'll look at a variety of social media platforms. If your goal is the widest possible distribution of your music, using multiple platforms is a good strategy.

YOUTUBE

YouTube is consistently one of the top five visited sites on the Internet. With your video on YouTube, you have access to a potential audience of billions. You also have the possibility of gaining subscribers to your channel, so your fans will be automatically notified when your next video comes out. And if enough people view your videos, you can also earn ad revenue.

To maximize your exposure, uploading your music video to YouTube is necessary, but not sufficient—it's a crowded market and standing out can be difficult when every other music act on the planet is uploading to YouTube too. There are a few basic requirements to get as many views as possible.

First, make sure your video's metadata (information about the video)—the title, description, thumbnail, and tags—are as complete as they can be. Extensive metadata help potentially interested viewers find you. If they are browsing in YouTube, searching through search engines, or scanning thumbnails, good metadata will get them to your video more quickly, while bad or missing metadata may mean they never find it.

Title

This is the most basic label for your video, but sometimes artists don't provide all the relevant information in the title: the name of the artist, the name of the song, and if a cover, the name of the original artist. If you have notable guest performers in the video, include them in the title as well.

Description

The description should include as much relevant information as possible about the song. Search engines will find your music video more easily if the description includes details like the following:

- The names of all the performers
- The names of the people (and companies) involved in the production of the music video
- The dates and locations of the music video
- Links to your other social media accounts
- The lyrics, if applicable
- Any short stories or explanations about the song, the filming, etc.

It's possible to have a description that's too long, but usually the problem is that it's too short. A detailed description can help search engines find your video, but it can also help build fans as they learn more about you and your song and make a stronger connection with your creativity and your music.

Just be sure you don't "spam" the description field—fill it full of popular tags and phrases that have nothing to do with your song, hoping more people will find it. If you don't get penalized by YouTube for having misleading information, which may result in having your video removed, you'll at least annoy a lot of people who thought they were getting something different. You're unlikely to build a good fanbase by trying to trick people into watching your video.

Thumbnail

When browsing through possible videos to watch, a potential viewer sees the thumbnail first, and that will sometimes be enough to get them to watch. It's worthwhile to make sure the thumbnail photograph is eye-catching and simple, with good exposure and composition that will do its best to grab the audience. Usually the thumbnail should be the most compelling shot in the video, although customizing or modifying the shot—for example, to include the song title—can be a valuable strategy as well. The band Walk Off The Earth does a great job of consistently creating thumbnails with bright colors and the song title to catch a viewer's attention.

Tags

As with other metadata, include as many tags as possible as long as they are relevant to the video. Tags can include the artist's name, musical genres, narrative themes (such as "love story"), film style ("film noir"), techniques used in the video ("stop motion"), primary color palette, and anything else that can legitimately describe an aspect of the song or the video.

FACEBOOK

Facebook is another one of the consistently top-five websites. YouTube videos can be linked to appear in Facebook feeds, but uploading a video directly to Facebook is often a valuable strategy for increasing exposures for your music, particularly if there's a strong Facebook following for your band.

YOU NEED TO KNOW HOW TO REACH THE RIGHT PEOPLE. THIS IS AN ONGOING LESSON FOR ME. FIRST, THINK ABOUT HOW PROFESSIONAL THE WORK IS AND BE HONEST WITH YOURSELF. THEN DECIDE ON WHAT PLATFORM THE VIDEO BELONGS (YOUTUBE, INSTAGRAM, FACEBOOK ETC.); THIS DEPENDS ON WHERE YOUR COMMUNITY EXISTS. THEN TARGET. FACEBOOK HAS SOME GREAT TOOLS TO DO THIS, WHICH IS A WHOLE COURSE IN ITSELF.

–Steve Umculo, South African Musician and Entertainer

On the one hand, if you just post a link to your YouTube channel on Facebook, it's a way of driving traffic to your YouTube site and promoting your YouTube channel. On the other hand, the absolute number of views your music video gets may be less than if you upload directly to Facebook, since it's easier to view and share native Facebook videos. You should decide if the goal is to maximize video views (and song plays), regardless of the platform, or if it is to get people to your YouTube page, to increase views and subscribers there.

VIMEO

Vimeo rarely has the viewer numbers YouTube does, but many creators prefer the channel because of its more artsy reputation and its lack of advertisements. Vimeo viewers tend to give more supportive feedback, while YouTube viewers with negative opinions typically don't hesitate to share them. Vimeo also has a cleaner layout and the ability to update a video without losing views of the original.

While Vimeo does offer free accounts for video uploaders, they are limited, so Vimeo creators are more likely to pay for a subscription. YouTube allows almost unlimited uploads, but users pay for the privilege with ads, which may show before, during (at the bottom), or after your music videos.

The guidelines for Vimeo metadata are similar to those for YouTube (above). Be as clear and complete as possible, maximizing the possibility of others finding your video.

INSTAGRAM

Time limits on Instagram videos mean you can't show a full music video there, but the platform can still be an effective way to promote a video on other channels. Create "teaser" (preview) videos of your song, behind-the-scene snippets, and other shorter videos for promoting your song, your brand, or your channel. You can't link from the video itself or in the description to a full version of the video, but you can direct people to look at your profile, which can include a live link to YouTube or some other channel.

The description for an Instagram post is not generally very long, so don't include as much detail as your YouTube description. But you can and should include as many hashtags as are relevant, so other Instagram users can easily find you.

TWITTER

If you have an active following, Twitter is another good way to promote a video. In a tweet, embed a link to a video hosted on another site, such as YouTube or Vimeo.

OTHER WAYS TO USE YOUR MUSIC VIDEO

- If your band has a website, include your music videos on it. Generally, these will be embedded videos hosted on either YouTube or Vimeo.

- If you are performing in a live show, have your videos available to play at the venue, such as in the lobby before the show or on an onstage screen during breaks.

- For your emails, create an email signature that includes a thumbnail and a link to your latest video.

- Pick your favorite two- or three-second clip from the video, make it into an animated gif (for example, using the gif maker on giphy.com), and send the gif when texting.

As new social media platforms emerge, there will be new ways to share. Once you have the goal in mind, you'll see new opportunities everywhere you look.

LIVE STREAMING

Besides using your polished music video in creative ways, don't forget to use more spontaneous video on any of these platforms as another way of connecting with your fans. From Alek Palmersmith, a musician and university music professor:

> IN THE MUSIC ENSEMBLE I TAUGHT, THE STUDENTS WOULD OFTEN SET UP A PHONE ON A MUSIC STAND, AND SIMPLY LIVE STREAM A SONG TO SOCIAL MEDIA PLATFORMS. I HAVE A LOT OF FRIENDS IN BANDS THAT DO THIS FOR PARTS OF REHEARSALS (INCLUDING INTERACTING WITH FANS DURING BREAKS) AND LIVE SHOWS.

DISTRIBUTION AND PROMOTION AT A GLANCE

YouTube

- Title
- Description
- Thumbnail
- Tags

Facebook

Vimeo

Instagram

Twitter

Other ways to use your music video

Live streaming

FINAL THOUGHTS

WITH A LITTLE BIT OF KNOWLEDGE ON MUSIC VIDEO PRODUCTION AND CAMERA USE, YOU CAN VERY EASILY TAKE YOUR VIDEO FROM BAD TO GOOD. HOWEVER, TO TAKE IT FROM GOOD TO GREAT IS A LONGER ROAD THAT REQUIRES DEEPER STUDY.

—Eli Gauden, Norwegian Singer-Songwriter

You've now read through a lot of detail, and it might seem overwhelming to take it all in. The important thing is to just get started: Art creation is messy, but it gets better the more you do it.

MY WORK EXPLORING MUSIC VIDEO PRODUCTION HAS GIVEN ME THE CONFIDENCE TO GO CREATE SOMETHING—IT'S EASY TO GET TOO BOGGED DOWN IN INFORMATION WITHOUT PUTTING IT INTO PRACTICE, SO I REALLY LIKE THE PUSH TO COMPLETE A VIDEO. IT WAS LIBERATING TO REALIZE THAT INTERESTING CONTENT CAN BE MADE WITHOUT A HUGE BUDGET.

—Alek Palmersmith, Musician, Educator

I hope this book helps you on the road to making your own music videos. If all goes well, you may get to the point where you can afford to have other people make all your music videos, which makes perfect sense, but there is great satisfaction from doing it yourself – or at least being closely involved in the process.

YOU ALREADY SEE THE VISION AND YOU ALREADY KNOW HOW THE STORY ENDS. YOUR AUDIENCE IS COMING FROM A BLANK SLATE. YOUR JOB IS TO LEAD YOUR AUDIENCE THROUGH THE DARK AND INTO THE LIGHT. IF THEY DON'T SEE THE LIGHT AT THE END, THAT ISN'T ON THEM—IT'S ON YOU!

—Dav Abrams, Musician

I have benefited greatly from the insights and perspectives of those who have contributed their ideas to this book: many former students, colleagues, and friends at Berklee, and various musicians and music video producers throughout the world, including some I have never met, who responded to my cold-call email asking for their thoughts about making music videos. I'm grateful for this community and for their willingness to share their experiences. They have enriched my knowledge, and this book is stronger for their contributions.

With that in mind, I'll end with one more quote from former student Steve Umculo, who has a great way with words (and a fierce dedication to making fascinating DIY music videos):

CREATIVITY IS A FUNNY THING. THE WORLD TENDS NOT TO TAKE IT TOO SERIOUSLY (AND MAYBE FOR GOOD REASON), BUT WHEN YOU'RE IN THAT MOMENT AND YOU FIND YOUR GROOVE, IT'S THE ONLY THING YOU WANT TO DO. IF AN IDEA SWEEPS YOU AWAY THEN IT'S IMPOSSIBLE NOT TO SEE IT THROUGH. IT'S MOST CERTAINLY NOT THE EASIEST THING TO DO, MY BELOVED READERS, BUT I WOULD TAKE THESE MOMENTS OVER A DESK JOB ANY DAY OF THE WEEK. NOW GO FORTH AND BE CREATIVE. THE WORLD NEEDS IT!

CONTRIBUTORS (IN ALPHABETICAL ORDER)

Dav Abrams is a musician who pioneered innovative 360-degree video techniques while in the masters program at Berklee Valencia. He also studied at Rutgers University and Rochester Institute of Technology.

Nick Clark is a producer, director, and editor whose work has encompassed film, TV, and web. He has collaborated with cutting-edge institutions like Berklee College of Music, ubiquitous brands including Staples and ConEdison, and iconic performers like Judy Collins and Melissa Ferrick.

Audio visual artist and songwriter **Anjie Concepcion** has made it her mission to spark conversations by exploring elements of fear, fun, love, and loss through colorful expressions in film and music. While pursuing degrees in Music & Film Production from Miami-Dade College and Berklee College of Music, she collaborated in various video productions. To explore more of her work visit www.anjieconcepcion.com.

Earlybird (Dana Fakhoury) is a Lebanese electronic/indie pop music producer. Coming from a graphic design background, she has followed her passion for music, as a guitarist in a band, then traveling around the world pursuing workshops and courses, and finally receiving a master's degree in Music Production Technology and Innovation at Berklee College of Music in Valencia, Spain.

Lisa Forsyth is an artist who works in both traditional and digital media. Her illustrations appear in Chapter 2.

Eli Gauden is a Norwegian singer-songwriter and performing artist who is active in the pop-folk music scene in Norway. Nominated for the Best Massachusetts Solo Artist Award, she has received both the Jack Perricone Award and the Movement Award from the Berklee College of Music. She studied at Berklee College of Music in Valencia, Spain. She is also a former Norwegian cast representative at *Up With People*. Look for Eli Gauden on YouTube.

Stephen "Steve Umculo" Haiden is a musician, entertainer, and ball of energy. An independent artist from Johannesburg, South Africa, Steve travels the world spreading messages of positivity with his music. He graduated with his masters in Contemporary Performance from Berklee College of Music (Valencia, Spain) in July, 2017, and has since grown his singer-songwriter project, Steve Umculo, into a full-time career.

Michael Sean Harris is a Jamaican vocalist, electronic musician, and educator, as well as a vocal coach and adjudicator for televised talent competitions *Digicel Rising Stars* and *All Together Sing*, respectively. He is a former Dean/Director of Studies of the School of Music at the Edna Manley College of the Visual and Performing Arts, Kingston, Jamaica.

Oliver Kersey is a British singer-songwriter currently composing and performing in the United States. He has headlined in front of an audience of 10,000, and has performed alongside Andy Grammer, T-Pain, Us the Duo, and Silentó. He has had airtime on the BBC, and his music was featured in the soundtrack of the film *Let it Go*. Gravity Castle is his latest endeavor with former bandmate Gabriel Gledhill.

Kasia Kijek and **Przemek Adamski**, Polish film directors and animators, have been winning film and animation awards for more than a decade. They have been honored with a Best Animation and a Grand Prix award from the Yach Film Festival, with an Antville Music Video Award, and with awards from the Annecy International Film Festival, CutOut Fest, LA Film Fest, D&AD slice, Animafest, and KTR gold. See samples of their work at kijekadamski.com.

John C. Leavitt is an active composer/arranger/pianist working in both the United States and Europe. Raised in Colorado, he enjoys traveling, and finds inspiration in nature and in experiences lived with others. Samples of John's work can be found on YouTube by searching "John C. Leavitt."

Laser Malena-Webber is one half of the Doubleclicks. Both a musician and music video director, she has directed music videos for a handful of other music acts, and is the author of a forthcoming book about crowdfunding for Berklee Press/Hal Leonard. The Doubleclicks videos currently have 3.7 million views. More than 125 of their videos can be found at youtube.com/thedoubleclicks.

Spencer Malley is a musician pursuing a degree in music education at the University of Connecticut, and plans to become an elementary music teacher. He is currently working on *Mass of Christ the King*. He studied Music Video Production at Berklee College of Music in Valencia, Spain.

Gregory Ohrel and **Lionel Hirlé** (Gret et Lio, Paris) are French film directors and photographers with wide experience employing interesting visual effects and creating riveting narrative videos. They are the creators of the Jain music videos with over 200 million views. For Jain's Makeba video, they received a 2017 Art Directors Club Silver Cube award, given for excellence in craft, design, and innovation.

Musician and educator **Alek Palmersmith** has 11 years of experience in the music industry, and six years teaching at the university level. Alek currently lives in Los Angeles where he works as a freelance recording and mixing engineer.

Savannah Philyaw is an indie-folk singer-songwriter from San Diego, CA. She recently completed a collection of songs for Warner Bros. TV Productions and has had her songs played on Cartoon Network, KPBS, Radio Rock 92.6 The Blitz, and AVRadio. Having shared the stage with some of her biggest influences – such as Jason Mraz, Kate Voegele, and Howie Day – she continues to perform at various venues in Southern California. She is a graduate of Berklee College of Music with a degree in music business.

Christos Stylianides is a professional music producer and mixing engineer from Cyprus. His obsession for high-quality audio has excited him to study audio engineering and music production. His primary task is helping artists turn their demos and recordings into finished records.

Shaudi Bianca Vahdat is an Iranian-American musician and theatre artist exploring story-driven songwriting through influences that include musical theatre, jazz, classical, and American and Iranian folk music. She is an actor (BA in Drama Performance, University of Washington) and vocalist (Master of Music in Contemporary Performance, Berklee College of Music). Her work can be found on both Spotify and iTunes. More at shaudibiancavahdat.com.

Josh Wallace is a dynamic composer, singer, and percussionist. He graduated with a Masters of Arts in Contemporary Performance (Production Concentration) from Berklee Valencia in 2018, and holds a Bachelor of Arts in General Music (Percussion Emphasis) from BYU Hawaii.

Pierce Warnecke is a sound and video artist who works equally in the sonic and visual domains creating performances, installations, and compositions. His works have been commissioned by CTM Festival, Deutschlandradio Kultur, ORF Musikprotocoll, and Mirage Festival. He was invited by Berlin's Institute for Sound and Music to create visuals on the Hexadome project at Martin Gropius Bau Museum (featuring Brian Eno, Thom Yorke, Holly Herndon, Ben Frost, et al.). He teaches Music Production, Technology, and Innovation at Berklee College of Music in Valencia, Spain.

Stephen Webber is an Emmy-winning composer, producer, engineer, multi-instrumentalist, and music innovator. He is the composer and turntable soloist of the Stylus Symphony, a groundbreaking work that combines a full orchestra with hip-hop, trip-hop, and dubstep, and is responsible for expanding Berklee's curriculum to include music video production, surround mixing, DJing and turntablism. The author of books on DJing and turntable as an instrument, he has appeared in *The New York Times* and *Rolling Stone*, and has written dozens of articles for *Mix Magazine*, *Remix*, and *Electronic Musician*. He is currently the executive director of BerkleeNYC.

Naomi Westwater Weekes is a singer-songwriter and producer based in the Boston area. Mixing organic Americana and electronic indie, her imaginative stage presence, intimate lyrics, and emotive voice inspire and provoke audiences. For more information, visit naomiwestwater.com.

Soo Wincci is an award-winning singer, recording artist, actress, and composer, as well as a former Miss World Malaysia. She has a PhD in business administration, and is currently a fellow at the Berklee College of Music in Valencia, Spain.

Simon Yu is a musician, editor, and music video director with a degree in contemporary writing and production/performance from Berklee. In addition to making music and music videos, he owns a production company in New York City (simonyuproduction.com), and has worked with artists and labels such as Snarky Puppy, Brass Against, Yo-Yo Ma's Silk Road Ensemble, Lucky Chops, Jojo Mayer's Nerve, GroundUp Music, Ropeadope Records, and Greenleaf Music.

ABOUT THE AUTHOR

Jon Forsyth created the curriculum and taught the first music video production courses for the Berklee College of Music, at both their Valencia, Spain and Boston, MA campuses. He currently spends half of each year in Valencia, helping students increase their understanding and skills, getting involved in extracurricular music (he made a great Man of La Mancha in the Broadway Showcase), and improving his beach volleyball skills. In addition to developing video innovations (like twin blade and metronome stop-motion animation techniques), Jon is a sculptor and photographer, and his video art has been featured several times on the marquee of the Boston Convention and Exhibition Center. He holds an MBA from the Wharton School, University of Pennsylvania. (jonforsyth.com)

MUSIC BUSINESS MUST-HAVES

ALL YOU NEED TO KNOW ABOUT THE MUSIC BUSINESS – 8TH EDITION

by Donald S. Passman
Free Press

The definitive and essential guide to the music industry, now in its eighth edition – revised and updated with crucial information on the industry's major changes in response to rapid technological advances and economic uncertainty.

00119121 ....$32.00

ENGAGING THE CONCERT AUDIENCE

by David Wallace
Berklee Press

Learn to engage, excite, captivate and expand your audience! These practical techniques will help you to communicate with your listeners on a deeper, more interactive level. As you do, the concert experience will become more meaningful, and the bond between you and your audience will grow.

00244532 Book/Online Media $16.99

HOW TO GET A JOB IN THE MUSIC INDUSTRY – 3RD EDITION

by Keith Hatschek with Breanne Beseda
Berklee Press

This third edition includes a new career tool kit and social media strategy. Inside you'll find: details on booming job prospects in digital music distribution and music licensing; interviews with nine music industry professionals under 35 who discuss how they got their starts, plus what skills today's leading job candidates must possess; and much more.

00130699 ....$27.99

MANAGING YOUR BAND – SIXTH EDITION

ARTIST MANAGEMENT: THE ULTIMATE RESPONSIBILITY

by Stephen Marcone with David Philp

From dive bars to festivals, from branding and merchandising to marketing and publicity, from publishing and licensing to rights and contracts, Marcone and Philp leave no stone unturned in this comprehensive guide to artist management.

00200476 ....$34.95

MELODY IN SONGWRITING

by Jack Perricone
Berklee Press

Discover songwriting techniques from the hit makers! This comprehensive guide unlocks the secrets of hit songs, examining them, and revealing why they succeed. Learn to write memorable melodies and discover the dynamic relationships between melody, harmony, rhythm, and rhyme.

50449419 ....$24.99

MUSIC LAW IN THE DIGITAL AGE – 2ND EDITION

by Allen Bargfrede
Berklee Press

With the free-form exchange of music files and musical ideas online, understanding copyright laws has become essential to career success in the new music marketplace. This cutting-edge, plain-language guide shows you how copyright law drives the contemporary music industry.

00148196 ....$19.99

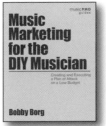

MUSIC MARKETING FOR THE DIY MUSICIAN

by Bobby Borg
Music Pro Guides
Music Marketing for the DIY Musician is a proactive, practical, step-by-step guide to producing a fully integrated, customized, low-budget plan of attack for artists marketing their own music.

00124611 ....$29.99

MUSIC MARKETING

by Mike King
Berklee Press

Sell more music! Learn the most effective marketing strategies available to musicians, leveraging the important changes and opportunities that the digital age has brought to music marketing. This multifaceted and integrated approach will help you to develop an effective worldwide marketing strategy.

50449588 ....$24.99

PAT PATTISON'S SONGWRITING: ESSENTIAL GUIDE TO RHYMING – 2ND EDITION

Berklee Press

If you have written lyrics before, even at a professional level, you can still gain greater control and understanding of your craft with the exercises and worksheets included in this book. Hone your writing technique and skill with this practical and fun approach to the art of lyric writing.

00124366 ....$17.99

THE PLAIN AND SIMPLE GUIDE TO MUSIC PUBLISHING – 3RD EDITION

by Randall D. Wixen

In this expanded and updated third edition, Randall D. Wixen adds greater depth to such increasingly important topics as the rapidly shifting industry paradigms, the growing importance of streaming and subscription models, a discussion of new compulsary license media, and so much more.

00122219 ....$24.99

SONGWRITING: ESSENTIAL GUIDE TO LYRIC FORM AND STRUCTURE

by Pat Pattison
Berklee Press

Veteran songwriter Pat Pattison has taught many of Berklee College of Music's best and brightest students how to write truly great lyrics. Her helpful guide contains essential information on lyric structures, timing and placement, and exercises to help everyone from beginners to seasoned songwriters say things more effectively and gain a better understanding of their craft.

50481582 ....$16.99

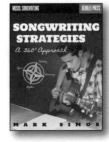

SONGWRITING STRATEGIES

by Mark Simos
Berklee Press

Write songs starting from any direction: melody, lyric, harmony, rhythm, or idea. This book will help you expand your range and flexibility as a songwriter. Discussions, hands-on exercises, and notated examples will help you hone your craft. This creatively liberating approach supports the overall integrity of emotion and meaning in your songs.

50449621 ....$24.99

HAL•LEONARD®

www.halleonard.com

Prices, content, and availability subject to change without notice.